The Book On BS

Fog of Deception:
Unmasking the BS in Modern Life

The Book On Series

Taylor Reed

Published by The Book On Publishing, 2025.

First edition. October 29, 2025

Website: https://thebookon.ca

Substack: https://thebookonpublishing.substack.com/

The Book On BS: Fog of Deception: Unmasking the BS in Modern Life

First edition. October 29, 2025

ISBN: 978-1-997909-49-1

Written by Taylor Reed

Other Books in The Book On Series

The Book On Life Unscripted
The Book On Risk Management in Payments
The Book On AI for Everyday People
The Book On Relationships
The Book On Master The Algorithm
The Book On Saying No
The Book On Community-Led Strategy
The Book On The Myth of Multitasking
The Book On The Burnout Blueprint
The Book On The Digital Reboot
The Book On The Shape of What's Coming
The Book On Strategic Obsession
The Book On High-Stakes Thinking
The Book On Artificial Leverage
The Book On Clarity
The Book On Uncertainty
The Book On Operational Excellence
The Book On Escape
The Book On Reinvention After Consequences
The Book On Re-Unifying Society
The Book On Taking Flight
The Book On Persuasion
The Book On Enough
The Book On Attention

Table of Contents

CHAPTER 1: THE ANATOMY OF BS 9

THE MECHANICS OF MODERN BS..10

THE ECOSYSTEM THAT FEEDS IT 12

THE INTERNAL DIMENSION 14

WHY WE CAN'T JUST STOP 15

THE EPISTEMIC COLLAPSE 18

THE EXHAUSTION FACTOR 20

THE RECOVERY QUESTION 22

CHAPTER 2: THE HISTORICAL ROOTS OF DECEPTION 24

THE ANCIENT PRECEDENT: RHETORIC AS POWER 24

MEDIEVAL AND EARLY MODERN DECEPTIONS 27

THE RISE OF MODERN ADVERTISING: MANUFACTURING DESIRE............29

POLITICAL PROPAGANDA: THE TWENTIETH-CENTURY REFINEMENT.......32

THE DIGITAL AMPLIFICATION: INFRASTRUCTURE FOR INFINITE BS 35

CHAPTER 3: CONFIDENCE VS. COMPETENCE.......................38

THE DUNNING-KRUGER INDUSTRIAL COMPLEX 39

THE CERTAINTY PREMIUM IN CAPITAL ALLOCATION 41

CONFIDENCE AS CURRENCY IN CRISIS..43

THE CREDENTIAL PARADOX 44

THE PERFORMANCE REVIEW ECONOMY..46

WHY COMPETENCE CAN'T COMPETE..47

THE SURVIVOR'S EDIT 49

THE REPLICATION CRISIS IN CORPORATE KNOWLEDGE.....................50

SKIN IN THE GAME AS CONFIDENCE SUPPRESSANT...........................52

CHAPTER 4: THE CULT OF AUTHENTICITY 54

THE RAW STORY INDUSTRIAL COMPLEX..55

CORPORATE AUTHENTICITY THEATER 57

THE AUTHENTICITY PREMIUM AND CLASS SIGNALING 59

THE PARADOX OF AUTHENTIC SCALE 61

THE AUTHENTICATION INDUSTRIAL COMPLEX 63

THE EXHAUSTION ECONOMY 65

WHEN AUTHENTICITY BECOMES GATEKEEPING 66

THE WAY OUT ISN'T BACK 68

CHAPTER 5: POLITICAL FOG 71

THE PLAUSIBLE DENIABILITY MACHINE 72

THE FOCUS GROUP FEEDBACK LOOP 74

THE SPECTACLE SUBSTITUTION 77

THE EXPERT CAPTURE PROBLEM 79

THE OUTRAGE INDUSTRIAL COMPLEX 82

THE ACCOUNTABILITY VACUUM 84

CHAPTER 6: INFLUENCER CULTURE: 87

THE PARASOCIAL CREDIBILITY TRANSFER 88

CREDENTIAL SIMULATION AND AESTHETIC EXPERTISE 90

THE CONTENT TREADMILL AND QUALITY DEGRADATION 92

MANUFACTURED RELATABILITY AND STRATEGIC VULNERABILITY 94

THE EXPERTISE MARKETPLACE AND MANUFACTURED CREDENTIALS 97

THE CRISIS OF SCALE AND OUTSOURCED AUTHENTICITY 99

ALGORITHMIC CAPTURE AND THE DEATH OF ARTISTIC RISK 101

CHAPTER 7: THE WELLNESS INDUSTRY 103

THE BIOMARKER OBSESSION AND QUANTIFIED SELF DELUSION 104

THE SUPPLEMENT INDUSTRIAL COMPLEX AND EPISTEMIC LOOPHOLES . 106

DETOX MYTHOLOGY AND THE PROFITABLE FICTION 109

THE GURU ECONOMY AND MANUFACTURED CHRONIC ILLNESS 111

BIOCHEMICAL INDIVIDUALITY AS UNFALSIFIABLE MARKETING 114

CHAPTER 8: CORPORATE SPIN 118

THE EBITDA SHELL GAME AND CREATIVE DEFINITION 119

THE STRATEGIC PIVOT AND RETROACTIVE VISION 120

THE MANUFACTURED CRISIS AND EXECUTIVE HEROISM.................. 122

THE ACQUISITION AS NARRATIVE RESET.................................... 125

THE PURPOSE-WASHING AND VALUES THEATER 127

THE GUIDANCE GAME AND EXPECTATIONS MANAGEMENT................ 129

CHAPTER 9: SELF-DELUSION **133**

THE NARRATIVE IMMUNITY SYSTEM... 134

THE RETROSPECTIVE REVISION ENGINE 136

THE EXCEPTIONAL SELF FALLACY.. 139

THE INTENTION-ACTION GAP AND ITS FICTIONAL BRIDGES 141

THE SUNK COST SANCTUARY AND THE STATUS QUO LOCK-IN 144

THE COMPARISON, MANIPULATION, AND SELECTIVE BENCHMARKING .. 147

CHAPTER 10: MEDIA NOISE.. **151**

THE VELOCITY PROBLEM AND RETRACTION ASYMMETRY 152

THE ATTENTION ECONOMY'S EXTRACTIVE LOGIC 155

ALGORITHMIC AMPLIFICATION AND THE MANUFACTURED CONSENSUS. 157

INFORMATION COLLAPSE AND THE IMPOSSIBILITY OF SHARED REALITY.. 160

CHAPTER 11: SPOTTING THE BS: A PRACTICAL GUIDE.......... **164**

THE CERTAINTY-COMPLEXITY MISMATCH...................................... 165

THE EVIDENCE SUBSTITUTION GAME 167

THE UNFALSIFIABLE PIVOT 170

THE COMPLEXITY CONCEALMENT PROBLEM 172

THE CONSENSUS FABRICATION.. 175

THE TEMPORAL DISPLACEMENT TRICK.. 177

THE CREDENTIAL MISDIRECTION 180

CHAPTER 12: BEYOND THE FOG... **184**

THE ECONOMIC COSTS OF VERIFICATION 185

EPISTEMIC LEARNED HELPLESSNESS AND THE RETREAT TO TRIBALISM .. 187

THE WEAPONIZATION OF DOUBT AND STRATEGIC UNCERTAINTY 189

BUILDING PERSONAL VERIFICATION PROTOCOLS............................ 192

DEVELOPING CALIBRATED SKEPTICISM... 193

THE SOCIAL COSTS OF TRUTH-SEEKING 196

Chapter 1: The Anatomy of BS: Understanding Its Core

BS isn't lying. That's the first thing you need to understand. A liar knows the truth and actively works against it; there's effort involved, intentionality, a relationship to reality, even if adversarial. BS operates in a different dimension entirely. The BSter doesn't care about truth or falsehood. Truth is irrelevant to the enterprise. What matters is effect, impression, the construction of a reality that serves an immediate need. When a founder tells investors their app will "revolutionize how humans connect," they're not lying because they haven't stopped to consider whether it's true. They're building a verbal structure designed to extract capital, and whether that structure corresponds to anything real is beside the point. This distinction matters because we've built entire social and economic systems that reward BS while punishing lies, as if the former were somehow more honest than the latter. It's not. It's worse.

The philosopher Harry Frankfurt got here first with his slim 1986 essay, but he wrote for academics, and the concept escaped containment. What he identified was a mode of speech and thinking that has metastasized into the default setting of modern discourse. Frankfurt argued that BS represents a greater threat to truth than lying because lies at least acknowledge truth's existence. The liar respects truth enough to oppose it. The BSter operates in a post-truth space where factuality is just one possible consideration among many, and usually not the most important one. In the decades since Frankfurt wrote, we haven't just tolerated this mode, we've professionalized it, systematized it, taught it in business schools and political campaigns. We call it "framing" or "messaging" or "personal branding," but the mechanism remains identical: the separation of speech from any accountability to reality.

The Mechanics of Modern BS

Watch how BS actually works in practice. A CEO stands before employees and declares, "We're not just a company, we're a family." This statement does not claim severance policies, healthcare coverage, or whether you'll be fired via Zoom. It's designed to generate a feeling, create an atmosphere, position the speaker as caring, and the organization as warm. Whether employees actually receive familial treatment is irrelevant to the BS's function. The statement succeeds if it produces the desired emotional response in the moment, even if that response contradicts material reality. This is BS in its purest form: language deployed for effect, untethered from any commitment to describe things as they are.

The machinery operates through several key mechanisms—first, confidence substitutes for competence. The person who speaks with certainty, who radiates assurance, who never hedges or qualifies, wins the room regardless of whether they know what they're talking about. We've trained ourselves to read confidence as expertise, conviction as knowledge. A financial advisor who says, "the market will definitely recover in Q3" sounds more authoritative than one who says, "historical patterns suggest volatility with multiple possible outcomes depending on interest rate decisions and geopolitical factors." The latter is more accurate. The former gets the client. Second, complexity becomes camouflage. The more intricate and technical the language, the harder it becomes to identify BS. Management consultants excel at this: they'll tell you about "synergistic optimization frameworks" and "value-add paradigm shifts" until your eyes glaze over. At that point, you assume they must know something you don't. The opacity is the product.

Third, and most insidiously, BS appropriates the language of authenticity itself. This represents a relatively recent evolution. Traditional BS was smooth, polished, and clearly performative. Modern BS comes wrapped in the aesthetic of realness. The influencer who posts crying selfies about their struggle with anxiety, while sponsored by a meditation app. The politician who says "I'm going to level with you" before delivering carefully focus-grouped talking points. The brand that promises to "keep it real" while its entire supply chain runs on exploited labor. This meta-BS is particularly effective because it pre-empts criticism. If you question it, you're accused of cynicism, of refusing to believe people can be genuine. The performance of authenticity has become so sophisticated that pointing out the performance makes you the asshole.

The Ecosystem That Feeds It

BS doesn't flourish in a vacuum. It thrives in environments where verification is difficult, consequences are delayed, and incentives reward short-term impression management over long-term accuracy. Silicon Valley built an entire economic model on this foundation. A startup raises millions on a pitch deck full of "projected growth curves" and "addressable market size" calculations that have no relationship to anything that will actually happen. The founders aren't lying; they genuinely don't know whether their projections are accurate, and more importantly, they don't need to know. What matters is securing this round of funding. By the time reality fails to match the projection, the narrative has shifted to "pivoting" or "evolving the model" or, if things go badly enough, "learning experiences for next time." The system absorbs the disconnect between claim and reality as a feature, not a bug.

Social media accelerated this dynamic into overdrive by removing even the minimal gatekeeping that previously existed. Anyone can declare expertise, and the platforms reward confidence and engagement rather than accuracy. A person with no medical training can amass millions of followers by posting confidently about "toxins" and "cleanses" while actual doctors struggle to compete because their careful, hedged, evidence-based communication doesn't generate the same emotional response. The algorithms don't care about truth; they care about engagement, and BS engages. It makes people feel certain, scared, or inspired, which are all high-engagement emotional states. Nuance and epistemic humility are low-engagement states. The economic incentives actively select for BS and against accuracy.

This creates what we might call the BS industrial complex: an interconnected network of industries, institutions, and individuals whose economic survival depends on maintaining BS's legitimacy. Management consultants need organizations to believe that success comes from adopting the right framework rather than executing obvious fundamentals. Wellness influencers need people to think that health comes from purchasing specific products rather than sleeping enough and moving regularly. Political campaigns need voters to believe that complex policy problems have simple solutions that align conveniently with tribal identities. Publishers need authors to claim their books contain revolutionary insights rather than competent syntheses of existing knowledge. None of these groups can acknowledge that most of what they sell is BS, because their business models depend on sustaining the impression of unique value.

The Internal Dimension

The most uncomfortable truth about BS is how much of it we produce ourselves, for our own consumption. Self-deception represents a particularly virulent strain because it faces no external opposition; there's no one to call you out when you're lying to yourself. We tell ourselves stories about why we deserve success we haven't earned, why our failures aren't our fault, why this time will be different despite identical circumstances to last time. This internal BS serves a protective function. Reality often hurts. Admitting we're not as talented as we believed that we made preventable mistakes, that we're not special, these truths threaten the ego structure we've built. BS provides cushioning.

Consider the person who repeatedly commits to lifestyle changes, exercise, diet, productivity systems, with genuine conviction each time, only to abandon them within weeks. Are they lying to themselves when they declare, "This time I'm really going to stick with it"? Not exactly. In the moment of declaration, they feel the conviction. The feeling is real. But there's a kind of willful blindness to the pattern, a refusal to integrate past evidence into current belief. This is BS's internal form: the mind constructing a narrative that serves immediate emotional needs without regard for whether that narrative corresponds to behavioral reality. We do this constantly, about ourselves and our lives, because the alternative, clear-eyed assessment of our actual patterns and limitations, is difficult to sustain.

The most sophisticated internal BS involves meta-narratives about our own honesty. We tell ourselves, "I'm the kind of person who tells it like it is" or "I don't play games, I just keep it real." These self-concepts allow us to BS with a clean conscience because we've pre-identified as non-BSters. The person who prides themselves on "radical honesty" but carefully curates which truths they share and which they conceal. The individual who claims to "hate drama" while reliably creating it. The professional who considers themselves "data-driven" but cherry-picks which data to consider. These people aren't hypocrites in the traditional sense; they genuinely believe their self-narratives. That's what makes the BS so durable. It's protected by layers of self-concept that make questioning it feel like attacking your identity.

Why We Can't Just Stop

If BS is this pervasive and destructive, why don't we simply commit to truth-telling? Because the costs of truth in a BS-saturated environment are real and immediate, while the benefits are diffuse and delayed. Tell the literal truth in a job interview, including your actual weaknesses, real reasons for leaving previous jobs, and an honest assessment of your skill gaps, and you won't get hired. The person willing to BS smoothly about their "passion for the mission" and "proven track record" receives the offer. Be genuinely honest in dating apps about your flaws, uncertainties, and relationship baggage, and you'll get fewer matches than someone projecting uncomplicated confidence and curated success. This isn't because people prefer lies, it's because BS has become the expected language of self-presentation, and speaking a different language marks you as either naive or deficient.

Organizations face similar constraints. A company that communicated honestly about risk, uncertainty, and the limits of its knowledge would get destroyed by competitors willing to project certainty. Investors don't want to hear "we think there's a reasonable chance this might work if several factors align favorably." They want to hear "we're going to dominate this market." The incentive structure rewards BS at every level. Politicians who speak carefully about policy trade-offs lose to those who promise simple solutions. Media outlets that present nuanced analysis lose audience to those that provide clear villains and heroes. Educational institutions that acknowledge the uncertainty in their fields lose prestige to those that project authority. The rational individual response to these incentives is to BS, even if the collective outcome is a degraded information environment where nobody can trust anything.

This creates what game theorists might call a BS trap: a situation where individual incentives drive behavior that produces collectively terrible outcomes, but no individual can afford to defect from the pattern. The tragedy is that we mostly recognize this. Most people, if you talk to them privately after drinks, will admit that much of professional discourse is performative BS. They'll acknowledge that most meetings could be emails, that most mission statements are meaningless, and that most claims of innovation are repackaging. But this private knowledge doesn't translate into public behavior because the costs of being the first to stop BSing are too high. You need coordination, collective action, new norms, and institutions. Until then, we're stuck playing a game where everyone knows the rules are stupid, but nobody can afford to stop playing.

The anatomy of BS, then, reveals not just a phenomenon but a system, one that has become load bearing in our economic and social structures. It's not enough to identify BS or even to understand how it works. We need to confront why it persists, what functions it serves, and what would be required to build systems that reward accuracy over impression. That investigation requires us to look more carefully at the specific domains where BS has achieved market dominance, and to understand the particular mechanisms by which it captures entire fields. But first, we need to accept the uncomfortable reality: we're not just victims of other people's BS. We're participants in the system, beneficiaries of it, and producers of it ourselves. The BS is coming from inside the house.

The Epistemic Collapse

Here's what happens when BS achieves critical mass: we lose the ability to distinguish it from legitimate discourse. Not because we're stupid or lazy, but because the distinguishing features erode. Real expertise starts by adopting BS's aesthetic because that's what gets heard. Actual innovation borrows BS's language because that's what gets funded. Genuine insight packages itself in BS's wrapper because that's what penetrates the noise. The result is a form of epistemic pollution where the signal-to-noise ratio degrades so completely that even careful observers can't reliably separate substance from performance.

Consider academic publishing, which was supposed to be the bastion against exactly this kind of degradation. The peer review process, the citation systems, and the tenure requirements are all designed to ensure that only verified knowledge progresses. Yet academia has produced its own species of BS, one that's arguably more pernicious because it comes wrapped in the garments of rigor. Researchers p-hack their way to publishable results, running experiments until they get statistically significant findings through sheer chance. They chase trendy topics not because the questions matter but because that's where the grant money flows. They write papers structured less around discovery and more around the formula that journal editors accept. This isn't fraud; nobody's fabricating data. It's BS: the systematic prioritization of publication over truth, career advancement over accuracy, the appearance of science over its substance.

The replication crisis revealed the extent of the damage. When researchers actually tried to reproduce published findings in psychology, they succeeded less than half the time. These weren't fringe studies; these were papers in top journals, findings that had been cited thousands of times, results that had made it into textbooks and informed policy. The BS had been credentialed, peer-reviewed, and institutionally validated, and it still didn't correspond to reality. What failed wasn't just individual researchers, but the system designed to catch exactly this kind of failure. And here's the uncomfortable question: if the institutions specifically built to resist BS have been compromised, what chance do less rigorous domains have?

The answer, based on available evidence, is none. Every field that lacks immediate feedback mechanisms, where you can BS without reality contradicting you quickly, has been colonized. Strategic consulting thrives despite no evidence that organizations that hire consultants outperform those that don't. The self-help industry generates billions while life satisfaction metrics stagnate or decline. Financial advisors charge fees for portfolio management that consistently underperforms index funds. These aren't marginal phenomena. They're enormous industries built on the proposition that expertise exists where it demonstrably doesn't. The reason they persist isn't that people are fooled; it's that the BS serves other functions. Hiring a consultant gives executives political cover for unpopular decisions. Buying a self-help book provides the feeling of working on your problems without the discomfort of actually changing. Paying a financial advisor offers the illusion of control in a fundamentally uncertain domain. The BS isn't incidental to these transactions; it's the product being sold.

The Exhaustion Factor

There's a reason this chapter keeps returning to systems and incentives rather than individual failures. It's because the most corrosive effect of pervasive BS isn't that it misleads people, it's that it exhausts them. Maintaining vigilance against BS requires constant cognitive effort. You have to verify claims, check sources, consider incentives, resist emotional manipulation, and question confident assertions. Do this for every piece of information you encounter, and you'll never do anything else. Nobody has that kind of energy. So we develop heuristics, shortcuts, rules of thumb about what to trust and what to dismiss. And BSters, consciously or not, optimize for those heuristics.

They learn that citing studies, any studies, regardless of quality, grants legitimacy. That confident body language overcomes weak arguments. Aligning with existing tribal beliefs provides protective cover against scrutiny. That complexity intimidates, where clarity might expose. These aren't sophisticated strategies. They're basic pattern exploitation. But they work because the alternative is expecting everyone to perform PhD-level critical analysis of every claim they encounter, which is absurd. The exhaustion creates surrender. People retreat to trusted sources, which increasingly means sources that confirm what they already believe. The breakdown in shared epistemic standards isn't mainly about polarization or filter bubbles; it's about the cognitive impossibility of maintaining BS resistance at scale.

This exhaustion extends beyond information consumption into self-presentation. Everyone knows you're supposed to brand yourself now. Curate your LinkedIn, manage your online reputation, craft your narrative, tell your story. This requires you to BS about yourself constantly, to present a coherent, confident, upwardly mobile persona regardless of how you actually feel or what your life actually looks like. The gap between the performed self and the experienced self generates its own pathologies. You start to forget which version is real. The performance becomes automatic, a second nature that's somehow more natural than your first. People report feeling like frauds, not because they're actually fraudulent, but because they've internalized the idea that the real them isn't good enough, that only the BS version deserves to exist in public space.

The cost of this perpetual performance is a kind of alienation from your own experience. You can't just do things anymore;

you have to consider how doing them will play, what narrative they'll fit into, and how they'll photograph. The experience itself becomes secondary to its representation. Travel influencers who spend trips staging photos rather than actually experiencing places. Parents who document their kids' lives more than they participate in them. Professionals who worry more about how work will look on their resume than whether the work is worth doing. This isn't shallow narcissism, or not only that. It's a rational response to an environment where the representation often matters more than the reality, where the story you tell about your life has more impact on your opportunities than the life itself.

The Recovery Question

If we're this deep in the BS, institutionally, socially, psychologically, what would recovery even look like? You can't simply decide to start telling the truth, because as we've established, unilateral truth-telling in a BS-saturated environment just means losing to people who maintain the BS. You can't reform institutions one at a time, because BS institutions outcompete honest ones in the short term. You can't rely on education, because the educated are often the most sophisticated BSers, having learned to dress BS in credentialed language. The problem isn't that people don't know better. It's that knowing better doesn't provide an exit.

What makes BS so resilient is that it's not a deviation from normal operation; it's how the system achieves stability.

Remove the BS, and things break. Strip away overstated resumes and optimistic projections, and half of the economy seizes up. Demand rigorous honesty in political campaigns, and nobody could form coalitions. Require genuine authenticity in social relations, and most networking collapses. The BS isn't a bug in how we communicate. It's a load-bearing element of how modern social and economic coordination happens. That's why moral exhortations to "just be honest" are useless. The dishonesty isn't a personal failing. It's a structural requirement.

This doesn't mean recovery is impossible. It means recovery requires understanding what functions BS currently serves and building alternative mechanisms that serve those functions without the epistemic damage. That's harder than it sounds. Much harder. It requires institutional innovation, new incentive structures, and cultural shifts that don't happen by wishing. But the first step is recognizing that you can't think your way out individually. The BS trap is collective. Any exit has to be too.

Chapter 2: The Historical Roots of Deception

Deception didn't emerge with social media, nor did it begin with television advertising or political spin doctors. The mechanics we recognize today, the performance of certainty where none exists, the substitution of appearance for substance, the elevation of presentation over reality, have roots stretching back to the earliest moments of recorded human civilization. What has changed isn't the existence of BS but its acceleration, its legitimization, and most critically, its transformation from occasional tactic into structural necessity. To understand why we live in an age where BS has become ambient, the air we breathe, rather than the pollution we notice, requires examining how we got here. The story isn't one of moral decline or technological corruption. It's far more interesting and far more damning. It's the story of how human societies discovered that certain forms of deception could be systematized, professionalized, and eventually naturalized into the very architecture of power and commerce. The BS didn't win because it was more persuasive than the truth. It won because it was more useful.

The Ancient Precedent: Rhetoric as Power

The sophists of ancient Greece were the world's first professional BS artists, and they knew exactly what they were doing. They didn't pretend to seek truth; they explicitly marketed themselves as teachers of persuasion, how to make the weaker argument appear stronger, how to win debates regardless of the merits of your position. Plato despised them for this, writing dialogue after dialogue in which Socrates dismantles their techniques. But here's what Plato either missed or refused to acknowledge: the sophists thrived precisely because their service was more valuable than philosophy. In Athens, where legal cases were argued before citizen juries and political questions were decided in public assemblies, the ability to persuade mattered more than the ability to discover truth. A merchant accused of fraud didn't need Socratic wisdom. He needed Gorgias to teach him how to construct a compelling defense. The sophists understood something fundamental about human social organization that philosophers have spent millennia trying to wish away: in contexts where decisions are made collectively and quickly, the appearance of correctness beats actual correctness almost every time.

This wasn't a bug in Athenian democracy. It was a feature. Direct democracy, for all its philosophical appeal, created structural incentives for BS. When hundreds or thousands of citizens must make decisions about complex matters, military strategy, economic policy, and criminal justice, without time for deep investigation, persuasion becomes the primary mechanism of choice. The person who can generate the most conviction in the shortest time wins. Truth, which often requires nuance, qualification, and patience, can't compete. The sophists didn't corrupt a pure system; they correctly identified the system's actual operating principles and built a business model around them. They were the first to recognize that in large-scale human societies, the gap between what people need to believe and what they can actually know creates a permanent market for convincing-sounding filler. That market has never closed.

What made the sophists genuinely sophisticated, and what distinguishes them from mere liars, was their explicit awareness of what they were doing. They taught argumentation as a techne, a craft with its own rules and standards, divorced from the content being argued. A sophist could teach you to argue both for and against the same proposition with equal conviction because the skill being taught wasn't about believing anything. It was about generating belief in others. This is the original sin of professionalized BS: the moment deception becomes a teachable skill rather than a character flaw; it enters the realm of legitimate expertise. You can have master practitioners, advanced techniques, and professional standards. Once that happens, BS stops being something people do when they lack integrity and becomes something people do because they've been properly trained. The sophists made BS respectable by making it professional. Every PR firm, every advertising agency, every political consulting group that exists today is their direct descendant.

Medieval and Early Modern Deceptions: Institutional Authority

The medieval Church understood something the sophists didn't need to consider: when you control the means of knowledge production, you don't need sophisticated rhetorical techniques. You just need institutional authority. The Church claimed monopoly access to divine truth, and for centuries, that claim went largely unchallenged, not because it was persuasive but because challenging it was structurally impossible. Most people couldn't read. Those who could read couldn't access texts. Those who could access texts had been trained in institutions controlled by the Church itself. The brilliance of this system wasn't its arguments; medieval theology is often fantastically creative but wildly unconvincing, but its elimination of the conditions under which arguments could be evaluated. When you can't check the source material, when you can't consult alternative interpretations, when questioning itself is defined as sin, BS doesn't need to be convincing. It just needs to be official.

The sale of indulgences represents this system at its most nakedly transactional. The Church claimed that it could reduce your time in purgatory in exchange for money, a claim with no biblical foundation and no mechanism of verification. You paid. A priest wrote your name in a ledger. You were promised reduced suffering in an afterlife no one could observe or measure. This is BS elevated to a sacrament, the Church literally monetizing its control over meaning itself. What made this possible wasn't theological sophistication but institutional monopoly. The Church could make these claims because it was the only institution authorized to make claims about salvation. Challenging the claims meant challenging the institution, which meant challenging the entire social order it supported. The system protected the BS, which it helped maintain. This is the pattern that repeats throughout history: deception becomes structural when institutions gain the power to define what counts as truth within their domain, then use that power to protect claims that serve their interests.

The printing press didn't end this dynamic; it displaced it and multiplied it. Suddenly, anyone with access to a printing press could claim authority, could publish their interpretation of scripture, could present their version of events as definitive. The Protestant Reformation wasn't a triumph of truth over institutional deception; it was the fracturing of a monopoly on religious BS into competitive markets for religious BS. Now you had multiple groups claiming exclusive access to divine truth, each with its own institutional structures, its own authorized interpreters, its own mechanisms for dismissing alternative views as heresy. The proliferation of printed material meant more information was available, but it also meant more BS was available, and crucially, it became harder to distinguish between them. When you have one authoritative source, you know where the BS is coming from. When you have dozens, each claiming to be the one true source, the very concept of authoritative truth begins to dissolve. The information revolution of the sixteenth century created the conditions for our current information crisis: too many competing truth-claims, insufficient mechanisms for adjudication, and audiences forced to make choices based on factors other than accuracy.

The Rise of Modern Advertising: Manufacturing Desire

The twentieth century industrialized BS through advertising, transforming it from a tactic used by institutions claiming authority into a comprehensive system for manufacturing desire itself. Edward Bernays, Freud's nephew and the founder of modern public relations, explicitly theorized this transformation. In his 1928 book "Propaganda," Bernays argued that democratic societies required the "engineering of consent", systematic manipulation of public opinion by those who understood the psychology of crowds. His insight was that you don't persuade people by appealing to their reason or their conscious desires. You create associations that bypass reason entirely, linking products and ideas to deep psychological needs that people can't articulate and may not even recognize they have. This wasn't traditional deception, where you make false claims about your product. This was something more fundamental: creating the need the product supposedly fills.

Bernays demonstrated this in 1929 when he orchestrated the "Torches of Freedom" campaign to increase cigarette smoking among women. Smoking was considered unfeminine, so Bernays hired fashionable women to march in the New York City Easter Parade while smoking Lucky Strike cigarettes, which he framed as "torches of freedom" symbolizing liberation from male oppression. He tipped off the press, who covered the march as a spontaneous demonstration of feminist independence. Women didn't start smoking because they were convinced cigarettes were good for them. They started smoking because Bernays successfully linked cigarettes to freedom, liberty, and modernity, concepts with powerful emotional resonance that had nothing to do with tobacco. The brilliance of this approach is that you can't refute it by pointing to facts. Cigarettes objectively don't make you free, but that's not the claim. The claim is that smoking expresses freedom, signifies liberation, and communicates your modern identity. Facts can't touch that because it operates in the realm of meaning and symbolism, not empirical reality.

This technique metastasized throughout consumer capitalism because it solved a fundamental problem: how do you sell things to people who don't need them? You can't compete on utility alone once basic needs are met. You need to sell identity, status, belonging, self-actualization, concepts that are infinitely expandable because they're never fully satisfied. Modern advertising doesn't tell you a car gets good gas mileage. It tells you the vehicle expresses who you truly are, that driving it will make you feel alive, and that owning it signals success to others who matter. None of these claims can be proven false because none of them are empirical claims. They're invitations to participate in shared fantasies about what products mean. The product itself becomes secondary to the symbolic system surrounding it. This is why luxury brands can charge thousands for handbags that cost dozens to manufacture; they're not selling leather and stitching; they're selling admission to a social reality were owning that handbag matters. The BS is the entire system, not any specific claim within it.

What advertising proved was that BS could be engineered according to psychological principles, tested through market research, refined through repeated campaigns, and ultimately systematized into a permanent feature of economic life. By the mid-twentieth century, major corporations employed entire departments devoted to nothing but the production and distribution of carefully crafted BS. They hired psychologists to understand how people think. They hired artists to make the BS aesthetically compelling. They hired media buyers to ensure the BS reached the maximum number of eyes. They created award ceremonies to celebrate the best BS of the year. An entire professional class emerged whose job was to make people want things they didn't need by creating associations that bypassed rational evaluation. This professionalization is critical because it means BS was no longer something individuals did when they lacked scruples. It became something organizations did because it was good business, something professionals did because they'd been trained in the techniques, something society rewarded with wealth and status. The infrastructure for mass-produced BS was now in place.

Political Propaganda: The Twentieth-Century Refinement

Suppose advertising showed how to manufacture desire; political propaganda in the twentieth century showed how to manufacture reality itself. The totalitarian regimes of the 1930s and 1940s understood that if you control information flow completely enough, you don't just influence what people believe, you shape what they can conceive of believing. The Nazi Ministry of Propaganda under Joseph Goebbels and the Soviet apparatus under Stalin weren't primarily concerned with making persuasive arguments. They were concerned with eliminating alternatives to their preferred narrative. This required more than censorship. It required the active production of a complete explanatory system that could account for everything people experienced while directing attention away from anything that contradicted the official story. When food shortages happened under Stalin, they weren't evidence of failed economic planning; they were evidence of sabotage by enemies of the people. When military campaigns failed under Hitler, they weren't evidence of strategic mistakes; they were evidence of betrayal by internal enemies. Every outcome could be absorbed into the narrative because the narrative was designed to be unfalsifiable.

George Orwell understood this mechanism when he described "doublethink" in "1984", the ability to hold two contradictory beliefs simultaneously and accept both. But doublethink isn't just a feature of totalitarian psychology. It's a feature of any system where institutional power depends on assumptions that contradict observable reality. You see it in corporations that simultaneously claim to maximize shareholder value while insisting they care deeply about employee well-being and social responsibility. You see it in universities that claim to pursue truth while implementing policies designed to protect certain ideas from examination. You see it in individuals who claim to value authenticity while carefully curating their social media presence. The mechanism isn't primarily cognitive; it's social and structural. Doublethink works because you need to believe contradictory things to successfully navigate institutions that demand those beliefs. The punishment for failing to perform the required doublethink isn't logical inconsistency; it's social and professional exclusion.

What democracies learned from totalitarian propaganda wasn't the specific techniques; they didn't need secret police or state-controlled media, but the underlying principle: you don't need to control information completely if you can overwhelm people with so much contradictory information that they can't distinguish truth from BS. This is the discovery that enabled contemporary BS to flourish. In the Cold War, both the United States and the Soviet Union invested heavily in propaganda. Still, the American approach was more sophisticated precisely because it operated in an environment where information flowed more freely. Rather than eliminating alternative narratives, American propaganda simply ensured that preferred narratives were better funded, more widely distributed, more professionally produced, and more aligned with existing cultural assumptions. The Voice of America didn't need to lie about Soviet repression; Soviet repression was real, but it carefully omitted comparable American actions in Latin America, Africa, and Asia. The BS wasn't in any specific false claim but in the systematic imbalance of coverage that created an incomplete picture while seeming to offer comprehensive information.

This sophisticated approach to propaganda became the template for modern information management. You don't need to eliminate opposing viewpoints if you can marginalize them, defund them, or simply drown them out with higher-budget alternatives. You don't need to censor inconvenient facts if you can contextualize them in ways that minimize their significance or distract attention toward more emotionally compelling but less important stories. Contemporary political communication operates on this principle: control what people pay attention to, and you control what they think is important, regardless of what's actually important. The twenty-four-hour news cycle, with its emphasis on breaking news and trending topics, is the perfection of this approach. Events that should matter, slow-moving policy changes, long-term environmental shifts, and gradual erosions of rights get ignored because they can't be packaged as dramatic moments. Meanwhile, events that shouldn't matter, celebrity scandals, manufactured controversies, and symbolic gestures dominate coverage because they generate attention. The medium itself has become a BS-amplification device, rewarding whatever generates immediate engagement while systematically underweighting what requires sustained attention.

The Digital Amplification: Infrastructure for Infinite BS

The internet didn't create BS, but it removed the last constraints on its production and distribution. For most of human history, producing and distributing information required resources, printing presses, broadcast licenses, and distribution networks. These resources were scarce enough that they imposed quality filters, not because the people controlling them were more honest but because they had reputational capital to protect and competitors waiting to expose obvious falsehoods. The internet eliminated these constraints. Anyone can publish anything at any time to a potentially global audience at essentially zero marginal cost. This democratization of information production is celebrated as enabling free speech and diverse perspectives, which it does. But it also allows the industrialization of BS at a scale previously impossible. You can now generate thousands of pieces of content, test them against different audiences, optimize for engagement, and scale up whatever works, all within hours and all without any institutional gatekeeping.

Social media platforms accelerated this process by designing algorithms that optimize for engagement rather than truth. Facebook's News Feed doesn't show you what's most accurate or most important; it shows you what you're most likely to click, share, or comment on. These aren't the same thing. Content that triggers strong emotional reactions, outrage, fear, excitement, and tribal affiliation generates more engagement than content that requires careful thought or admits complexity. The platforms know this. Internal research from Facebook revealed that their algorithms were amplifying divisive content and misinformation because that content generated engagement. They made minor adjustments but kept the fundamental system because engagement is what they sell to advertisers. This means BS that provokes outrage will always outcompete truth that requires nuance in algorithmic distribution. The infrastructure itself is designed to amplify BS because the business model requires it.

What makes this particularly insidious is that the platforms can honestly claim they're neutral, they're just showing people what people want to see. But "what people want to see" is partly a function of what they've been trained to like through the algorithm's reinforcement patterns. If you consistently see content that triggers strong reactions, you get conditioned to seek that stimulation. If nuanced analysis gets buried in your feed, you stop expecting or valuing it. The algorithm shapes desire, then claims to be merely responding to desire. This is BS, recursively generating the conditions for more BS. We're not just swimming in a sea of deception; we're in an ocean where the currents themselves are designed to amplify and accelerate the deception, where the infrastructure rewards BS more than truth, and where the people controlling the infrastructure insist they're just giving us what we want. They're technically correct, but they're lying about how we came to like it.

Chapter 3: Confidence vs. Competence: The Power of Persuasion

We've engineered ourselves into a peculiar predicament: the people who know the least speak with the most certainty, and the people who know the most hedge every statement with caveats. This isn't an accident of personality distribution. It's a structural feature of how modern institutions select, reward, and elevate people. The confident incompetent rises while the competent skeptic stays put, not because organizations prefer failure to success, but because they can't tell the difference until it's too late. By the time reality catches up to performance, the confident performer has already moved on, leaving wreckage and a promotion in their wake.

The mechanism behind this inversion operates through what we might call "perceived competence arbitrage." In any domain where outcomes are delayed, ambiguous, or difficult to attribute to individual action, which describes most white-collar work, observers must rely on proxies for competence. They can't directly measure your grasp of supply chain optimization or market dynamics or regulatory compliance, so they measure what they can: how you talk about these things. Your fluency. Your certainty. The absence of visible doubt. This creates a perverse selection pressure where the appearance of mastery outcompetes actual mastery, because the former is immediately legible while the latter reveals itself only across time horizons that exceed most people's tenure in any given role.

Consider the architecture of the modern job interview, that bizarre ritual where strangers meet in artificial conditions to predict future performance through present conversation. The candidate who says, "I architected a complete digital transformation of our legacy systems, resulting in a forty-seven percent efficiency gain" gets further than the candidate who says, "I worked with a team to modernize some outdated processes, though measuring the exact impact is complicated because multiple factors were changing simultaneously." The first statement could be complete fiction, grandiose exaggeration, or legitimate achievement; the interviewer has no efficient way to distinguish between these possibilities. The second statement is almost certainly more accurate in its acknowledgment of complexity and uncertainty, but it sounds weaker. It sounds like someone who doesn't know their own value. In a thirty-minute conversation, certainty reads as competence. Qualification reads as doubt. And doubt, we've decided, disqualifies.

The Dunning-Kruger Industrial Complex

The most confident people in any room are usually operating at one of two extremes: genuine expertise or genuine ignorance. The psychological research here is worth examining, not because it explains everything, single studies explain nothing, but because it points toward something reproducible across contexts. David Dunning and Justin Kruger's work in the late 1990s demonstrated what many suspected: people with minimal knowledge in a domain consistently overestimate their abilities, while experts consistently underestimate theirs. The incompetent lack the metacognitive capacity to recognize their incompetence. They don't know what they don't know, so they feel no uncertainty.

But here's what matters for our purposes: we've built entire industries around this asymmetry. Management consulting doesn't thrive despite this gap between confidence and competence; it thrives because of it. A twenty-six-year-old associate with an MBA and two years of experience can walk into a manufacturing company that's operated for seventy years and, within weeks, deliver confident recommendations about restructuring their entire supply chain. They can do this not because they've achieved rapid expertise, but because they've been trained in the performance of knowledge. They know the frameworks, the terminology, the presentation templates. They know how to project certainty. The actual mechanics of supply chain management, the tacit knowledge that comes from years of navigating specific vendor relationships, understanding particular equipment constraints, and knowing which workers have which specialized skills, remain invisible to them. But it also remains invisible to the senior executives making decisions, who are themselves far removed from operational reality.

The consultants aren't frauds in the traditional sense. They believe their recommendations have value. They've been trained at elite institutions that taught them these frameworks work. But they've also been selected for their capacity to generate conviction, to walk into uncertain situations and impose clarity through sheer force of presentation. The client company doesn't hire consultants because it lacks smart employees who understand its own operations. They hire consultants because those consultants can deliver confident simplicity in contexts where their own employees would offer complicated reality. "It depends" doesn't justify a seven-figure engagement. "Here's exactly what you need to do.

The Certainty Premium in Capital Allocation

Watch how venture capital flows and you'll see confidence-competence arbitrage in its purest form. The founder who can tell a crisp, compelling story about inevitable market domination gets funded over the founder who offers a realistic assessment of challenges and uncertainties. This isn't because investors are stupid; most are quite intelligent within their domain. It's because in conditions of genuine uncertainty, which early-stage investing always involves, the ability to generate conviction becomes the primary signal. When you can't reliably predict which companies will succeed, and decades of VC returns show that even professionals mostly can't, you optimize for founders who make you believe they'll succeed.

Elizabeth Holmes at Theranos represents not an aberration but an exemplar of this dynamic. She raised hundreds of millions of dollars with technology that didn't work by perfecting the performance of inevitable success. The deep voice, the Steve Jobs turtlenecks, the board stacked with former cabinet secretaries and generals, these weren't incidental details. They were the substance of the offering. Investors couldn't evaluate the technology; almost none had relevant biotech expertise. What they could determine was the conviction of the presentation. Holmes never hedged, never qualified, never expressed doubt. She projected total certainty in contexts where even legitimate experts would feel uncertain. That certainty, far more than any technical demonstration, drove capital allocation.

The aftermath revealed something uncomfortable: many of the smartest investors in Silicon Valley, people whose entire profession involves evaluating early-stage companies, got comprehensively fooled by someone with no relevant expertise but exceptional performance skills. The standard response was "she was a con artist, an outlier, a cautionary exception." But the structural incentives that elevated Holmes remain unchanged. The next founder pitching a revolutionary technology still competes based substantially on performative certainty rather than demonstrable competence. The investors can't efficiently distinguish between the two, so they select for the signal they can measure: conviction.

Confidence as Currency in Crisis

The premium on confidence over competence amplifies during uncertainty. When institutions face genuine crises, financial collapse, pandemic, or military threat, the demand for decisive leadership intensifies. People want someone who knows what to do, even though the defining feature of a genuine crisis is that no one knows what to do. The information is incomplete, the situation is novel, and the interventions are untested. This is precisely when you need leadership that can tolerate ambiguity, update beliefs as evidence arrives, and acknowledge the limits of their knowledge. Instead, institutions systematically select for leaders who project unwavering certainty.

The 2008 financial crisis offers a catalog of this phenomenon. Lehman Brothers collapsed not because its executives lacked confidence, but because their confidence persisted well past the point where evidence should have shattered it. Internal emails show senior leadership dismissing warnings, insisting their risk models were sound, maintaining absolute certainty even as their positions deteriorated. This wasn't unique to Lehman; it was standard across the industry. The executives who expressed doubt, who suggested they might not fully understand the risks embedded in mortgage-backed securities, were viewed as insufficiently committed to the growth strategy. The ones who projected certainty got promoted, right up until the moment reality could no longer be outrun.

Similar patterns played out during COVID-19's early months. Public health officials faced a genuinely novel situation where key parameters, transmission rate, fatality rate, and mutation potential, remained unknown. The honest response would have been "here's what we know, here's what we don't know, here's our best guess with current information." Some officials tried this approach and were pilloried for sending mixed messages, for flip-flopping, for lacking leadership. Others learned to project confidence regardless of underlying uncertainty, to present preliminary findings as fact, to defend yesterday's recommendations even when new evidence suggested revision. The public, unable to evaluate epidemiological claims directly, defaulted to trusting whoever sounded most certain. Confidence became the measure of credibility.

The Credential Paradox

The most elaborate confidence games require the most impressive credentials. Elite education doesn't inoculate against BS, it professionalizes it. The Harvard MBA learns to call uncertain hunches "strategic insights." The McKinsey associate learns to present correlation as causation with enough technical complexity that clients can't easily challenge it. The published academic learns to frame exploratory data mining as hypothesis testing. These aren't cynical manipulations by bad actors. They're learned behaviors that institutions teach and reward.

Watch how credentials function in public discourse. When an economist makes confident predictions about policy impacts, the public weighs their Stanford PhD and their Federal Reserve experience against their track record of prior predictions. Except that no one maintains accessible databases of expert forecasting accuracy across time. The credential persists, the prediction failures fade. This creates a perverse incentive structure where being confidently wrong carries no penalty as long as you maintain institutional affiliation. The economist who predicted eight of the last three recessions keeps getting invited to share confident predictions about the next recession. Their continued presence in elite institutions signals competence to audiences who lack the time or tools to evaluate their actual record.

Medical specialists demonstrate this pattern starkly. Studies examining diagnostic accuracy show that specialists' confidence in their diagnoses often exceeds their actual accuracy. Radiologists viewing the same X-ray will reach different conclusions with equal confidence. But patients can't evaluate radiological competence directly; they rely on credentials and certainty. The radiologist who says, "this is definitely cancer" generates more trust than the one who says, "there's an ambiguous mass that could be several things; we need additional imaging." Both might be equally accurate in their ultimate diagnosis, but the confident one inspires more patient compliance and satisfaction. Medicine selects for this performative certainty through every stage of training and practice.

The Performance Review Economy

Corporate performance management systems function as confidence-detection machinery disguised as competence measurement. The annual review doesn't evaluate what you accomplished so much as how you frame what you accomplished. The employee who takes credit for team successes, who repackages routine work as innovative solutions, and who describes every project in language suggesting transformational impact scores higher than the one who accurately acknowledges collaborative effort, admits setbacks, and describes realistic incremental progress.

This isn't managers being fooled; they're often complicit. The manager who rates their reports highly looks better to their own superiors. They managed a team of high performers, evidence of their own leadership competence. Honest evaluation, acknowledging that most employees are, by definition, average, makes everyone look worse. So the system generates grade inflation, where outstanding performance becomes the default rating and actual underperformance gets coded in subtle language that maintains plausible deniability. The confident self-promoter who overstates their impact gets rated identically to the competent modest performer who understates it. Over time, this selects for confidence over competence at every organizational level.

The most successful corporate performers master a specific linguistic register: strategic ambiguity combined with projected certainty. They describe their work in terms abstract enough to resist falsification but concrete enough to sound substantive. "I drove cross-functional alignment to optimize our go-to-market strategy" could mean almost anything, from organizing a few meetings to leading a genuine organizational transformation. The ambiguity is the point. It allows credit-claiming for positive outcomes while maintaining distance from negative ones. And it sounds confident, professional, and leadership oriented. The person who says "I sent a lot of emails trying to get people to coordinate better, and it sort of worked" is describing potentially identical activity. Still, they're flagging themselves as lacking leadership presence.

Why Competence Can't Compete

The structural disadvantage of actual competence in modern institutions stems from a temporal mismatch. Confidence is immediately legible; competence reveals itself slowly. In the time it takes to demonstrate real expertise, the confident performer has already captured the room, secured the resources, and moved to the next opportunity. By the time their prior claims are exposed as overreach, they're no longer around to face consequences.

Real competence also tends toward qualification and nuance, which reads as weakness in environments optimized for decision speed. The expert acknowledges competing considerations, describes trade-offs, and expresses appropriate uncertainty about future outcomes. They've learned, through deep engagement with their domain, that most questions lack simple answers. This makes them poor performers in contexts that demand simple answers, which is most contexts where resources get allocated and decisions get made.

The truly competent also tend to underestimate the value of performance. They assume good work speaks for itself, that quality eventually gets recognized, and that substance matters more than style. These assumptions might have held in smaller organizations with longer tenure, where reputation could develop through extended observation. They fail comprehensively in large, fluid organizations where most interactions are brief, where people change roles every two years, and where your next boss has never seen your work and evaluates you based on how you present it.

This isn't a problem we can solve through individual virtue or better hiring practices. It's embedded in the architecture of how modern institutions operate. When you can't efficiently measure competence directly, you measure proxies. When those proxies favor confidence, you select for confidence. When you choose for confidence across decades, you build organizations led by people who are exceptional at projecting certainty and mediocre at everything else. The BS isn't a bug. It's what we optimized for.

The Survivor's Edit

Here's what makes the confidence-competence inversion nearly impossible to correct: the people best positioned to fix it are those who benefited from it most. The executive suite doesn't fill with introspective reformers questioning their own ascent. It is filled with people whose entire career trajectory validated the importance of confident self-presentation. They got here by doing exactly what the system rewards. Asking them to dismantle that system is asking them to retrospectively delegitimize their own success.

Consider the CEO who rose through sales, a domain where confidence directly produces results regardless of underlying product quality. They learned, correctly within their context, that belief generates outcomes. The best salespeople genuinely convince themselves of what they're selling; the confidence isn't fake; it's metabolized self-persuasion. When this person reaches executive leadership, they apply the same mental framework to strategic decisions. Project confidence, inspire the organization, and make people believe in the vision. Doubt becomes disloyalty. Questioning becomes negativity. They're not consciously choosing performance over substance; they can't distinguish between the two anymore. Their entire neural circuitry has been wired by decades of reinforcement that confidence produces results.

The same pattern holds for the management consultant who becomes Chief Strategy Officer, the investment banker who becomes CFO, the corporate lawyer who becomes General Counsel. Each rose through a profession where persuasion mattered more than prediction accuracy. They learned to present certainty in conditions of uncertainty, to frame partial information as complete analysis, to defend positions with conviction even when evidence was mixed. These weren't corrupt practices within their original contexts; they were core competencies. But they travel poorly to domains where reality imposes harder constraints than client perception.

The Replication Crisis in Corporate Knowledge

Academic research is finally reckoning with its replication crisis, the uncomfortable discovery that many published findings can't be reproduced. Corporate America needs a similar reckoning but will never get one, because companies don't systematically test whether their confident strategic decisions actually worked. The five-year plan gets announced with great certainty, resources get allocated, and initiatives get launched. Three years later, when market conditions have shifted and half the leadership team has turned over, no one conducts a rigorous post-mortem comparing predictions to outcomes. The new leadership announces its own confident strategy, and the cycle continues.

This creates perfect conditions for confidence to persist independent of competence. The executive who confidently predicted their digital transformation would increase efficiency by thirty percent never has to reconcile that prediction with messy reality. Maybe efficiency increased by fifteen percent, but three other variables changed simultaneously, so causation is ambiguous. Maybe efficiency increased thirty-five percent, but the consulting firm that conducted the measurement had incentives to validate the initiative. Maybe efficiency declined, but by the time this became clear, the executive had moved to another company where they now confidently predict their next transformation will increase efficiency by forty percent.

Private equity offers a particularly pure example. PE firms evaluate target companies, identify operational improvements, execute their strategy, and then sell. Their returns get measured, certainly, but measuring whether their specific operational interventions caused value creation versus whether they just benefited from multiple expansions and favorable exit timing requires analytical rigor that most firms don't apply to their own performance. The PE partner who confidently diagnosed problems and prescribed solutions gets validated by the exit price, regardless of whether their diagnosis was accurate or their solutions were what actually drove value. They take that validation to the next deal, where they apply similar confidence to different circumstances. The system selects for people who can generate conviction, not people whose prior convictions proved accurate.

Skin in the Game as Confidence Suppressant

Nassim Taleb's "skin in the game" framework offers one of the few structural solutions to confidence-competence inversion. When people face meaningful personal consequences for being wrong, their calibration improves rapidly. The trader who bets their own money learns to distinguish between confident intuition and actual edge. The surgeon who gets sued for malpractice learns appropriate humility about diagnostic certainty. The contractor who warrants their work learns realistic timelines and cost estimates.

But most modern white-collar work has successfully externalized consequences. The strategic consultant's recommendations fail? The client organization bears the cost while the consultant adds another case study to their portfolio. Does the economist's policy prescription cause harm? They write an article explaining why the implementation deviated from their advice. Does the executive's acquisition destroy value? They depart with a severance package worth more than most people earn in a lifetime. Does the corporate lawyer's advice expose the company to liability? The company pays the settlement, and the lawyer remains a partner.

This separation between decision-making authority and outcome responsibility creates space for unlimited confidence. You can be wrong repeatedly without personal cost, so there's no feedback mechanism to suppress overconfidence. The institutional incentive runs entirely in the opposite direction, toward projecting more certainty, claiming more credit, and accepting more responsibility (in title while deflecting it in practice). The person who says, "I'm not sure this will work" loses authority to the person who says, "I'm certain this will work," and neither faces meaningful consequences when it doesn't.

Chapter 4: The Cult of Authenticity: Marketing Fakery

The word "authentic" has become the most profitable adjective in modern commerce. Walk into any Whole Foods and count how many products promise authenticity, artisanal bread, authentic Mexican salsa, genuinely hand-crafted whatever. Open Instagram and watch influencers perform vulnerability like it's a choreographed dance number. Attend a leadership conference and listen to executives describe their "authentic selves" using language so identical that a single algorithm could've written it. We've created a market for realness so lucrative that faking authenticity has become the most valuable skill in the economy. The paradox doesn't trouble us. We've learned to perform sincerity, package spontaneity, and mass-produce the handmade. Authenticity stopped being something you are and became something you brand yourself as. The moment it became a commodity; it ceased to exist.

What makes authenticity-as-BS particularly insidious is that it's designed to be unfalsifiable. When someone claims to be authentic, what metric could prove them wrong? Traditional deception at least offered the possibility of factchecking; if you claimed your product cured cancer, someone could run tests. But authenticity operates in the realm of performed emotion and declared intention. A CEO stands on stage and says, "I'm just being real with you," and that statement becomes self-validating. To question it is to be cynical, jaded, and unwilling to connect. The accusation of inauthenticity becomes a greater sin than actual deception. We've built a rhetorical fortress where the performance of genuineness protects itself from scrutiny by labeling all scrutiny as an inability to recognize genuineness. It's an elegant trap. The person who sees through the performance gets cast as the one with the problem.

The Raw Story Industrial Complex

Consider the evolution of personal branding over the past decade. Early social media rewarded the highlight reel, perfect vacation photos, relationship milestones, and professional achievements, carefully curated for maximum status display. Then something shifted. The highlight reel got identified as inauthentic, and the market corrected. What replaced it wasn't actual authenticity but a more sophisticated simulation of it. Enter the "raw and real" post: the admission of struggle, the moment of vulnerability, the confession of imperfection. But watch the structure of these performances carefully. They follow a formula as rigid as any traditional advertisement.

The template goes like this: shocking admission of failure or pain (to grab attention and signal courage), brief wallowing in the difficulty (to establish emotional stakes and relatability), pivot to the lesson learned (to demonstrate growth and wisdom), closing statement of empowerment (to inspire the audience and reinforce the narrator's authority). You see it everywhere. "I lost everything in my twenties. I was sleeping on a friend's couch, questioning every decision I'd made. But that rock bottom taught me what truly matters. Now I help others avoid the mistakes I made." This isn't a vulnerability. It's the vulnerability-to-authority pipeline, a narrative technology for converting admitted weakness into demonstrated strength. The confession becomes credentials.

What makes this particularly effective is that it co-opts the language and emotional register of genuine self-disclosure. Real vulnerability, the kind that doesn't come with a lesson plan or a product tie-in, is messy, uncomfortable, and offers no resolution. It might be someone saying, "I don't know how to fix this, and I'm scared," and then just sitting in that fear without converting it into content. But that doesn't scale. It doesn't build a following. It doesn't lead anywhere marketable. So we've developed this parallel thing that looks like vulnerability and sounds like vulnerability, but functions as strategic self-marketing. The personal brand consultants will tell you explicitly: share your struggles, but make sure they're struggles you've overcome. Make sure the story has a redemption arc. Make sure the audience leaves inspired, not disturbed.

The influencer economy has industrialized this process to a degree that would make Procter & Gamble jealous. There are now courses teaching people how to "story-tell their authentic journey." Workshops on "vulnerable content creation." Guides to "sharing your truth in a way that converts." Notice how the language of therapy and self-help has merged seamlessly with the language of marketing and sales. Your trauma becomes your unique selling proposition. Your recovery becomes your product offering. Your ongoing struggle becomes your content calendar. And because it's all positioned as authentic self-expression, questioning it feels like attacking someone's lived experience. The commercial infrastructure gets protected by therapeutic language.

Corporate Authenticity Theater

The corporate version of this phenomenon might be even more absurd. Companies worth billions of dollars now employ teams of people whose job is to make the company seem like a person you'd want to be friends with. Brand voice guidelines specify how to sound "authentic" in customer service interactions. Social media managers are trained to deploy just the right amount of casual language and emoji to signal that the corporation isn't really a profit-maximizing entity but rather a quirky personality who happens to sell things. Wendy's Twitter account becomes known for snarky replies. Innocent Smoothies adopts a childlike whimsy. Every consumer-facing brand develops a human-sounding personality that's actually the output of a marketing department with quarterly targets.

The tell is always the consistency. Actual humans are inconsistent; we're tired some days, sharp others, occasionally contradictory, awkward, or inappropriately timed. But brand authenticity maintains perfect tonal control across thousands of interactions. It's authenticity with none of authenticity's defining features: unpredictability, genuine vulnerability, the occasional spectacular mistake that isn't immediately converted into a "we're owning it" meta-commentary. When a brand does screw up, watch how quickly it gets processed through the authenticity machine. Crisis PR teams now deploy the authentic apology template: acknowledge the hurt, express the learning, emphasize the values, and commit to doing better. The template is so standardized that you can spot it being used identically by a fashion company accused of racism and a tech company caught in a data breach. Same cadence, same vocabulary, same emotional notes. If that's authenticity, the word has lost all meaning.

What these companies understand, what they're betting their marketing budgets on, is that authenticity is no longer about being genuine. It's about following the signaling conventions that contemporary audiences have learned to recognize as markers of genuineness. It's performance in both senses: acting that's good enough to pass, and metrics that satisfy stakeholders. A brand can be "authentic" by the standards of brand authenticity without bearing any relationship to anything real about how the company actually operates, treats its workers, makes decisions, or pursues its interests. The brand is the performance. There's nothing behind it that could be authentic or inauthentic. It's a simulation all the way down, but because everyone's agreed to pretend otherwise, pointing this out makes you the problem.

The Authenticity Premium and Class Signaling

Here's what nobody wants to acknowledge: authentic consumption is how wealthy people distinguish themselves from strivers. The explosion of authenticity-branded products, farm-to-table restaurants, heritage-brand clothing, and small-batch everything coincides with a period of massive wealth inequality and class anxiety. When money alone can't signal status because too many people have access to mass-produced luxury, the wealthy shift to markers that require cultural capital to recognize an economic capital to access. That sourdough bread made from ancient grain varieties using traditional fermentation methods costs eight dollars for a small loaf. Still, you need to know why that matters to recognize the status it signals.

This is where authenticity's relationship to BS gets particularly tangled. The objects and experiences themselves might be real; that bread really was fermented for three days using a starter culture maintained for decades. But the meaning attached to them, the status they confer, the identity they construct for the consumer, that's all performance. You're not buying bread. You're purchase membership in a class of people who care about the right things in the right way. The transaction is authentic in its mechanics but BS in its function. And because it's all positioned as ethics and taste rather than status competition, questioning it becomes gauche. You're supposed to pretend everyone just naturally prefers artisanal products, as if the preference has nothing to do with what that preference communicates about who you are.

The wellness industry has perfected this mechanism. A seventy-dollar candle made from "sustainably harvested" materials with "essential oils chosen for their vibrational frequency" is selling authenticity as both a product attribute and a consumer identity. The person who buys it isn't just getting a candle; they're declaring themselves to be the kind of person who recognizes quality, values sustainability, and understands the connection between environmental consciousness and personal well-being. Whether any of this is true about the candle or the person doesn't matter. What matters is the signal. The purchase is the message. And because it's all coded in the language of personal values and conscious consumption, the commercial nature of the transaction gets obscured. You're not shopping, you're expressing your authentic self through mindful choices. The market thanks you for your authenticity.

The Paradox of Authentic Scale

The terminal problem with commodified authenticity reveals itself in the mathematics of scale. For something to be marketable, it must be reproducible. For something to be reproducible, it must be systematized. For something to be systematized, it must be formulated. But authenticity by definition resists formulation; the moment you can package it, it's not authentic anymore. This creates a permanent tension in the authenticity economy. Every successful authentic brand must eventually choose between staying small and genuine or growing large and simulated. The market pressures overwhelmingly favor the latter.

Watch what happens when an authenticity-based brand scales. The coffee shop that built its identity on personal relationships with customers opens a second location. The owner can't be at both places simultaneously. So they train managers to replicate the authentic vibe. They create guidelines for how staff should interact with customers, friendly but not forced, knowledgeable but not pretentious, and efficient but not rushed. They're literally writing a script for spontaneity. The third location requires hiring staff who have never worked at the original, so the "authentic vibe" gets transmitted through training materials and shift leader coaching. By the tenth location, authenticity has become indistinguishable from brand standards. Customers at location ten get the same performed warmth they'd get at any other trained-service establishment, but it's dressed in the language and aesthetics of the original authentic experience. The ghost of authenticity haunts the chain.

The same pattern plays out in personal brands that grow into media companies, in craft breweries that get acquired by conglomerates, in any authentic thing that success touches. There's an authenticity-to-scale pipeline, and it's perfectly efficient at converting the real into the simulated while maintaining the aesthetic markers of the real. The audience usually accepts this trade because they don't actually want the constraints of authentic scale; they want the feeling of genuine connection with the convenience of mass production. We want our favorite authentic musician to play the arena near us; not remain in dive bars we'd never visit. We want authentic style available in our size and budget, not limited to unique pieces we could never access. We want personality without the inconvenience of dealing with an actual person who might be unavailable, inconsistent, or difficult.

This is where we become complicit. We claim to value authenticity while consistently choosing its simulation. We say we want a real connection while optimizing for convenient interaction. We declare our preference for the genuine while rewarding the performed. The market gives us what we actually select for, not what we say we want. And what we choose for, through our clicks, purchases, follows, and attention, is authenticity that scales, productive vulnerability, and realness that comes with reliable hours and a return policy. We've created the demand that makes authentic fakery not just possible but necessary. The cult of authenticity thrives because we're all members, performing our membership while pretending we're just being ourselves.

The Authentication Industrial Complex

The irony thickens when you realize that distinguishing authentic from inauthentic has become its own profitable industry. We now have verification systems, certification programs, and expert consultants who validate authenticity for a fee. Blue checkmarks that confirm you're really you. Organic certifications that promise food is genuinely what it claims. Authenticity certificates for luxury goods prove they're not counterfeit. We've built an entire infrastructure around proving realness, which means realness itself has become something that requires institutional validation. If you need a third-party verification system to confirm authenticity, you've already admitted that authenticity isn't self-evident. It's not something you recognize through direct experience; it's something you trust because an authority stamped it.

This creates a peculiar dependency. The authentication systems gain power proportional to our inability to discern authenticity ourselves. The less we trust our own judgment, the more valuable the verifying institution becomes. It's in their interest for the landscape to be full of fakes, for the signals to be confusing, for the average person to feel overwhelmed by the possibility of deception. They're not just certifying authenticity; they're implicitly arguing that without certification, authenticity can't be trusted. The blue checkmark doesn't just verify identity; it suggests that unverified accounts are inherently suspect. The organic label doesn't just indicate farming practices; it implies that unlabeled food might be dangerous. We've outsourced the discernment of realness to systems that profit from our doubt.

And these systems are gameable. Every verification mechanism eventually gets captured by the thing it's supposed to verify. The organic certification process becomes complicated enough that large industrial farms can navigate it more easily than small farms that actually practice traditional agriculture. The authentic review system gets flooded with paid testimonials that follow templates designed to pass authenticity filters. The verification badge gets awarded based on criteria that favor institutional legitimacy over actual identity verification. The guardians of authenticity become the enablers of sophisticated inauthenticity. They're not preventing fakery, they're just raising the cost of entry, creating a barrier that well-resourced fakers can afford to cross while poorly resourced genuine articles get shut out.

The Exhaustion Economy

There's a toll to all this performance that nobody wants to calculate. Maintaining an authentic personal brand requires constant emotional labor, the work of seeming effortless, of appearing spontaneous on schedule, of being vulnerably available while protecting actual privacy. Social media creators talk about burnout, but they frame it as content creation fatigue. That's not quite right. The exhaustion comes from having to be performatively yourself all the time, from never getting to exist off-stage because your authentic self is your product, and the market never closes.

Watch what happens to people who build careers on authentic self-expression. They start out sharing what's genuinely on their mind, what they actually care about. It resonates because there's something real there, an actual perspective, an actual sensibility. But once it becomes their livelihood, they have to keep producing that realness on a schedule. Tuesday needs content. Friday needs content. The algorithm rewards consistency, so you can't just post when you genuinely have something to say. You have to have something authentic to express every forty-eight hours, and it needs to perform well enough to satisfy the metrics. Authenticity becomes a quota.

The psychological contortion this requires is rarely discussed honestly. You're mining your actual life for content, which means you start experiencing your life through the lens of its content potential. That difficult conversation with your partner becomes material. That moment of genuine joy gets interrupted by the thought of how to capture it. You're simultaneously living and representing living, and the two activities start interfering with each other. The authentic sharing that built your audience becomes a filter through which you experience everything. You haven't just commodified your personality, you've made surveillance of yourself a job requirement. The panopticon is now interior, and you're both guard and prisoner.

Some people break under this. They delete their accounts, disappear from public view, and talk about reclaiming their privacy and mental health. Good for them. But notice what happens next: the comeback. Six months or a year later, they return with content about their absence. The breakdown becomes the next arc in the authentic journey. "I had to step away to find myself again" becomes a TED talk about boundaries and self-care, which becomes a workshop series, which becomes a book about authentic living in the digital age. Even the rejection of the authenticity economy gets processed back into it. There's no outside. The exit is just another room in the same building.

When Authenticity Becomes Gatekeeping

The cult of authenticity has developed its own purity politics, and they're as vicious as any ideological enforcement mechanism. Communities built around authentic expression inevitably develop hierarchies of realness, where members compete to prove who's more genuinely committed, more truly aligned, more authentically themselves. The indie music scene ridicules bands that sign to major labels. The minimalist lifestyle community judges people whose minimalism includes too many expensive items. The body positivity movement questions whether conventionally attractive people can authentically participate. Every authenticity-based group eventually eats its own for insufficient authenticity.

This shouldn't surprise anyone. When your group identity is based on being more real than the mainstream, you need to constantly police the boundaries of that realness. Otherwise, what distinguishes you? If anyone can claim authenticity, the term loses its power as a marker of distinction. So you develop tests, shibboleths, ways of identifying the true believers from the posers. You create an authenticity hierarchy where you're never quite secure in your position because there's always someone who can claim to be more authentic, more dedicated, less compromised, further from commercial incentives. The quest for authentic community produces the opposite: a surveillance system where everyone watches everyone else for signs of inauthenticity, and the accusation becomes a tool for social control.

The cruelty here is that the people most vulnerable to these accusations are often the ones least equipped to defend themselves. Calling out inauthenticity becomes a way to police class, race, and cultural boundaries while claiming you're just protecting the integrity of the community. "That's not authentic punk" can mean "that's not working-class enough." "That's not authentic soul food" can mean "that's not Black enough." "That's not authentic craft" can mean "that's too accessible to normies." The language of authenticity provides cover for gatekeeping that would be indefensible if stated plainly. You're not excluding people based on identity or access, you're just recognizing what's real and what's fake. The judgment appears to be about the thing itself rather than who's producing or consuming it.

The Way Out Isn't Back

So, where does this leave us? The usual move here would be to call for a return to "real" authenticity; to suggest we can somehow recover genuine self-expression by being more mindful, intentional, or conscious of the performative traps. That's BS too. There's no return because there's no pure, authentic past we fell from. The idea that people in previous eras just naturally expressed themselves without performance is historical fantasy. Self-presentation has always been strategic. Identity has always been constructed. What's changed isn't that we've lost some natural authenticity; it's that the commercial infrastructure for packaging and selling performed authenticity has become sophisticated enough to recognize itself while continuing to function.

The way forward isn't backward to some imagined authentic existence. It's through to the other side of the authenticity discourse entirely. What if we stopped treating authenticity as the highest compliment? What if we recognized that all public self-expression involves performance and stopped pretending otherwise? Not as cynicism, but as clarity. You could perform a version of yourself knowingly, without the pretense that you're not performing. You could create content strategically without the therapeutic language, pretending it's just vulnerable sharing. You could buy products you like without the story that you're expressing your authentic values. The performance doesn't become less effective when you acknowledge its performance; it just becomes honest about what it is.

This won't happen at scale because too many people profit from the current arrangement. But individually, you can opt out of the game where you're constantly trying to prove your realness. You can let your contradictions stand. You can be calculatedly strategic about some things and genuinely spontaneous about others without pretending everything is one or the other. You can recognize that the person you are alone is different from the person you are with friends is different from the person you are professionally, and that's not inauthenticity, that's the normal complexity of being human in social contexts. The cult of authenticity wants you to believe there's one true self you're either expressing or betraying. There isn't. There are just versions you perform in different situations, some more conscious than others, all of them real in the moment you're doing them.

Chapter 5: Political Fog: Manipulation in Modern Governance

Representative democracy created a problem no ancient philosopher anticipated: the need to govern populations too large to gather in a single forum, making decisions too complex for any individual to fully comprehend, through representatives whose primary qualification is the ability to win elections rather than solve problems. This structural condition, representative distance combined with endemic complexity, generates an information asymmetry so profound that BS doesn't just fill the gap between governors and governed. It becomes the medium through which governance itself operates.

The politician stands before constituents who cannot possibly verify most of what gets said. They lack access to classified briefings, internal budget documents, lobbying conversations, and committee negotiations. They lack the time to read thousand-page bills, the expertise to evaluate economic projections, and the connections to confirm which version of events actually happened behind closed doors. The representative knows this. The voter knows this. And everyone proceeds anyway, engaging in a performance where persuasiveness substitutes for accountability because accountability requires information that deliberately remains unavailable. What emerges isn't occasional deception penetrating an otherwise honest system. It's a system where the architecture itself demands continuous manipulation simply to function.

The Plausible Deniability Machine

Watch how political language operates at the federal level and you'll notice something peculiar: it's been engineered for unfalsifiability. Statements get constructed not to communicate meaning but to create rhetorical escape routes. "We're taking this matter seriously" commits to nothing except the performance of concern. "We're exploring all options" sounds decisive while refusing any actual decision. "Mistakes were made," acknowledges error while erasing agency; mistakes apparently make themselves, no human hands required.

This isn't accidental imprecision. It's intentional vagueness refined over decades of damage control. Political consultants have developed a taxonomy of phrases that permit later reinterpretation regardless of what happens. Promise to "fight for" something rather than accomplish it, and you can claim victory whether the thing materializes or not; you fought, didn't you? Say you "take full responsibility" without specifying what consequences that responsibility entails, and you perform accountability while avoiding actual penalty. Announce you're "deeply troubled" by a revelation, and you signal concern without committing to action. The language creates a buffer zone between statement and reality wide enough to drive a policy reversal through if needed.

Legislative text perfects this erasure of meaning. Bills get titled with Orwellian precision: the "Patriot Act" curtails civil liberties, the "Clear Skies Initiative" loosened pollution restrictions, the "No Child Left Behind Act" effectively abandoned struggling schools. The names signal virtue while the mechanics do something else entirely, and by the time anyone reads the actual provisions, hundreds of pages drafted by lobbyists, amended in committee, passed at midnight, the branding has already won. Citizens end up defending or attacking laws based on their names rather than their contents because reading the contents requires legal expertise and forty hours nobody has.

But here's where it gets genuinely perverse: this isn't a bug that could be fixed with transparency requirements or plain-language mandates. The complexity is structural. Modern governance involves coordinating millions of competing interests through bureaucratic systems spanning thousands of agencies, implementing regulations across industries whose technical details require specialized knowledge, and allocating resources through budget processes where every line item represents someone's constituency. No human being can hold all this in their head simultaneously. No paragraph can accurately summarize a healthcare reform that affects insurance markets, Medicare reimbursements, drug pricing, medical device regulations, hospital networks, and state-level implementations differently across fifty jurisdictions.

So politicians simplify. They must. And in simplifying, they inevitably distort, not always maliciously, but necessarily. The question becomes: simplify toward what? Toward helping constituents understand trade-offs, or toward generating support regardless of understanding? The incentive structure points firmly toward the latter. A representative who says "This bill will help some people and hurt others, with effects we can't fully predict, and whether it's worth passing depends on values we disagree about" speaks truthfully but sounds weak. A representative who says "This bill will create jobs, lower costs, and protect our values" speaks falsely but sounds strong. Voters reward the second representative. Elections select for effective BSters, then give them power over complex systems where BSing becomes operationally necessary.

The Focus Group Feedback Loop

Political messaging no longer emerges from conviction and then seeks public acceptance. It appears from polling data, gets refined through focus groups, is tested across demographic segments, adjusted based on which phrases produce measurable persuasion gains, and finally delivered with performed conviction. This process inverts the relationship between belief and communication. The politician doesn't figure out what they think and then find words to express it. They find words that work and then adopt whatever thinking justifies those words.

Consider how policy positions shift within a single campaign. A candidate opposes an idea in the primary, where base voters demand purity, then moderates that opposition in the general election, were swing voters demand pragmatism. Ask whether their actual position changed, and you're asking the wrong question. Positions in this context aren't beliefs about policy; they're strategic responses to electoral incentives. The candidate performs opposition or support based on which performance best serves the goal of winning. What they personally believe, if they think anything beyond "winning is good," remains unknowable and irrelevant.

Frank Luntz pioneered the scientific approach to this manipulation, testing political language with the precision of pharmaceutical trials. His famous memo on climate change advised Republicans to emphasize "climate change" over "global warming" because focus groups found the former less frightening. He recommended calling inheritance taxes "death taxes" because the phrase generated negative reactions that the words "estate tax" didn't trigger. This wasn't wordsmithing for clarity. It was psychological engineering designed to create specific emotional responses regardless of accuracy. The inheritance tax applied to fewer than two percent of estates; calling it a "death tax" implied everyone faced it. But the deception worked because people don't fact-check their emotional reactions.

What makes this particularly corrosive is that both parties do it, just with different vocabularies. Progressives workshop terms like "reproductive freedom" and "undocumented immigrant" while conservatives workshop "pro-life" and "illegal alien", each side conducting focus groups to identify which frames generate desired responses from their targets. The result is a political discourse where nobody uses neutral language because neutral language has been scientifically proven to be less persuasive. We've optimized away honest communication in favor of maximum manipulation, and then we act surprised when voters feel manipulated.

The weapons laboratories for this linguistic engineering are polling firms and communications consultancies that treat voter psychology like a system to hack. They identify which demographics swing elections, determine what those demographics value, discover which phrases activate those values, and deploy those phrases with disciplined consistency until they saturate the information environment. When you hear the same talking points repeated verbatim across a hundred surrogates appearing on different networks, you're watching a coordinated deployment of focus-grouped language. The message didn't spread organically because it resonated. It spread because fifty operatives got the same memo and executed the same strategy.

The Spectacle Substitution

Governance requires tedious work: reading legislation, attending committee meetings, negotiating compromises, understanding budget implications, and evaluating policy outcomes. None of this generates compelling television. So politicians increasingly abandon governance for spectacle, the viral video, the theatrical hearing, the performative outrage, the symbolic gesture that accomplishes nothing but generates attention. The work gets delegated to staffers and lobbyists while elected representatives focus on being famous.

Congressional hearings demonstrate this perfectly. Watch contemporary committee sessions and compare them to hearings from thirty years ago. The format remains identical, representatives question witnesses under oath, but the function has inverted. Previously, questioners sought information. Now they seek clips. The five-minute question period gets used not to elicit testimony but to deliver a prepared statement disguised as questioning, with the witness functioning as a prop. "Isn't it true that your company..." isn't a question seeking an answer; it's an accusation optimized for later distribution across social media, edited to remove the witness's response.

Representatives know their questions in advance, coordinate with staff to prepare graphics and charts that will appear behind them, time their statements to conclude exactly when their period expires and immediately upload the video with a caption explaining what they "just destroyed" or "absolutely demolished." The hearing itself, the institutional purpose of gathering information to inform legislation, becomes secondary to the performance of the hearing, which exists to generate content for supporters and fundraising appeals for donors. Truth-seeking, in this context, becomes actively disadvantageous because genuine inquiry might lead somewhere unexpected, disrupting the narrative arc of the predetermined clip.

This substitution of spectacle for substance accelerates because spectacle metrics are immediate while substance metrics are delayed. A representative can see their video went viral within hours. Whether their policy improved lives might take years to determine, and attribution will remain contested. Immediate feedback shapes behavior more powerfully than distant outcomes, so the system selects for performers over legislators. The skills that win elections, charisma, message discipline, and theatrical presence, have essentially nothing to do with the skills that create effective policy: patience, technical knowledge, coalition-building, and compromise. But we keep using the former to select people for jobs requiring the latter, then wonder why governance fails.

The rise of the permanent campaign completes this transformation. Politicians used to campaign occasionally, then govern. Now they campaign continuously and govern incidentally. Every decision gets evaluated not for policy merit but for electoral impact. Every statement gets crafted not to inform constituents but to satisfy donors and activate base voters. Every appearance gets staged not to facilitate dialogue but to generate favorable coverage. This isn't corruption in the sense of illegal payoffs. It's structural corruption, the replacement of governance with performance art, where looking like you're solving problems substitutes for actually solving them.

The Expert Capture Problem

Democratic governance theoretically relies on expertise, elected generalists consulting with specialist experts who provide technical knowledge the generalists lack. But observe how expertise actually functions in political contexts and you'll find the relationship inverted: politicians don't consult experts to learn what's true; they shop for experts who will validate what's convenient. Climate scientists who endorse immediate, dramatic action get hired by one party; climate scientists who emphasize uncertainty and cost-benefit analysis get hired by the other. Economists who model minimum wage increases as job-killers find employment with conservative think tanks; economists who model them as poverty-reducers find employment with progressive ones.

This isn't experts corrupting politics. It's politics corrupting expertise. The think tank and advocacy organization ecosystem creates positions for credentialed academics willing to provide intellectual cover for predetermined conclusions. A representative can claim they're "following the science" or "listening to economists" while actually following whichever scientists or economists say what advances their agenda. The PhD becomes a prop, deployed to lend authority to partisan positions rather than constrain them.

What emerges is dueling expertise; on any contentious issue, you can find a qualified expert supporting any position. Want evidence that gun control reduces violence? Hire these researchers. Want evidence it doesn't? Hire those researchers. Need studies showing tax cuts boost growth? Commission these economists. Need studies showing they increase inequality without boosting growth? Commission those economists. The public watches experts contradict each other and reasonably concludes that expertise itself is BS, unable to distinguish between genuine scientific disagreement (which exists) and motivated reasoning dressed in academic robes (which dominates).

The most sophisticated version of this manipulation involves commissioning research with predetermined outcomes, which sounds impossible until you understand that study design determines results. If you want to "prove" that environmental regulations kill jobs, fund studies that measure only job losses in regulated industries while ignoring job gains in compliance, clean energy, and public health sectors. If you want to "prove" regulations create jobs, fund studies that measure the full employment impact. Both studies can be technically accurate while reaching opposite conclusions. The BS isn't in the methodology; it's in the pretense that you're discovering an answer rather than constructing one.

Government bureaucracies compound this problem through selective disclosure of internal research. Agencies conduct studies on policy effectiveness, environmental impact, and economic consequences, but release only findings that support their preferred outcomes. A Department of Defense analysis suggesting a weapons system is unnecessary gets classified; an analysis justifying it gets promoted. An EPA study finding minimal health risks from a chemical gets fast-tracked; one finding significant risks gets subjected to additional review. This isn't a conspiracy; it's an institutional incentive. The career official who produces research contradicting their agency's mission doesn't advance; the one who produces supportive research gets promoted. So, expertise within government becomes another tool for manufacturing justification rather than discovering truth.

The Outrage Industrial Complex

Effective governance requires calm deliberation, technical analysis, stakeholder compromise, and patience as policies get implemented and adjusted. None of these generates engagement. What generates engagement is outrage, the shocking revelation, the devastating scandal, the existential threat, the democracy-ending crisis. So political communications increasingly optimize for maximum outrage, transforming every policy disagreement into an apocalyptic battle between good and evil where compromise equals betrayal.

Watch the fundraising emails. They don't explain policy nuances or request support for incremental improvements. They scream emergencies. "We have just 24 hours to stop some catastrophe. "This is your FINAL CHANCE" to prevent disaster. "They want to DESTROY" everything you value. The language mimics emergency notifications, not because emergencies are happening, but because emergency language triggers immediate responses. Fear motivates action and donations more effectively than hope or reason.

This constant emergency footing corrodes the capacity for actual governance. When everything is an existential crisis, nothing is. When every vote represents the difference between freedom and tyranny, voters can't distinguish between consequential decisions and symbolic ones. When every opponent is evil rather than mistaken, compromise becomes impossible because you don't negotiate with evil. The outrage machine creates a political culture where solving problems matters less than demonstrating sufficient anger about them, were evidence of extreme emotion substitutes for evidence of sound judgment.

Social media amplifies this dynamic because outrage algorithms reward emotional intensity over factual accuracy. A measured thread explaining trade policy nuances might get a few hundred shares. A thread claiming trade policy represents betrayal by corrupt politicians in service to foreign interests gets thousands. The platform doesn't care which is true; it cares which generates engagement, because engagement creates advertising revenue. Politicians learn this quickly. The representative who posts sober analysis gets ignored; the one who posts inflammatory accusations gets amplified. So they post inflammatory accusations, the opposition responds with counteraccusations, and the cycle perpetuates until the entire information environment consists of people screaming past each other. At the same time, the actual policy happens elsewhere, negotiated by lobbyists that voters never see.

The media ecosystem reinforces this because conflict generates clicks while governing generates yawns. A bipartisan infrastructure bill that took months of negotiation and actually rebuilds bridges gets one story. A politician's inflammatory tweet about the other party gets five stories, three opinion pieces, and a week of cable news segments. News organizations aren't ignorant of this disparity; they're responding to it. They've learned that audiences reward coverage of conflict rather than coverage of governance, so they provide conflict. The representative seeking coverage quickly determines that doing their job effectively attracts less attention than picking fights strategically. Incentives align around producing spectacle, and governance becomes the thing that happens accidentally when spectacle participants aren't looking.

The Accountability Vacuum

Here's the culminating problem: democratic accountability theoretically operates through elections where voters evaluate representatives' performance and decide whether to return them to office. But this mechanism fails when voters lack information to assess performance, when attribution of outcomes to individual representatives proves impossible, when election timeframes misalign with policy timeframes, and when party loyalty overrides individual assessment. All four conditions now exist simultaneously.

Most voters can't name their House representative, much less evaluate what that representative accomplished during their term. They can't because the information required to make such an evaluation is not available. What did the representative vote for? What did those votes actually do? How did those policies affect outcomes? Which outcomes resulted from those policies versus other factors? This question is simultaneously unavailable and overwhelming. So voters default to party affiliation, national mood, presidential approval, and name recognition. The individual representative's performance becomes nearly irrelevant to their re-election chances, which means there's minimal electoral incentive to govern well and maximal incentive to maintain party loyalty and generate name recognition through spectacle.

Even for engaged voters attempting to hold representatives accountable, attribution proves nearly impossible. When unemployment drops or rises, which policies caused it? When infrastructure crumbles or improves, who deserves credit or blame? When healthcare costs shift, what role did legislation versus market forces play? The lag between policy implementation and observable outcomes spans years; the political memory spans months. A representative can vote for legislation that damages their district, get re-elected before the damage manifests, then blame the damage on their successor. Accountability requires connecting actions to outcomes, but the connecting mechanisms have been deliberately obscured.

Term limits were supposed to solve this by forcing regular turnover, but they've made it worse. Representatives facing term limits have even less incentive to govern responsibly because they won't face electoral consequences. Instead, they focus on positioning for their next career move, the lobbying job, the corporate board seat, the consulting contract. The system increasingly selects for people treating elected office as a brief credential-building stop rather than a long-term responsibility, which produces representatives optimizing for personal benefit rather than constituent welfare.

What we're left with is a system where BS isn't just tolerated but required. The representatives who succeed aren't those who govern best but those who perform best. The policies that pass aren't those that work best, but those that sell best. The information voters receive isn't accurate but optimized. And everyone involved, politicians, consultants, donors, media, even voters, has adapted to this reality so thoroughly that proposing actual accountability sounds naive. We've built a democracy that runs on manipulation, then wonder why trust in institutions collapses. The fog isn't an aberration penetrating political life. It is political life, and the only question that matters is whether we're still capable of imagining anything else.

Chapter 6: Influencer Culture: The Image Over Substance

The influencer economy runs on a spectacular inversion: people gain authority by demonstrating they have an audience, not by showing they know anything worth hearing. A twenty-three-year-old with two million followers giving financial advice has more cultural reach than an economist with forty years of research experience. A wellness influencer selling adaptogens and claiming they "fixed her hormones" gets more trust than endocrinologists who spent a decade in medical training. We've built a system where attention becomes its own credential, where the ability to gather eyes translates automatically into the presumption of expertise. The mechanism isn't accidental; it's the logical endpoint of a media environment that can't distinguish between popularity and authority because the metrics that measure both look identical. Views, shares, engagement rates, these numbers tell you how many people watched, not whether what they watched was true, useful, or anything more than elaborate performance art masquerading as guidance.

What makes influencer BS particularly efficient is its self-reinforcing loop. Traditional BS required some external validation; the consultant needed a company to hire them, the politician's votes required, and the charlatan customers needed. But influencers have discovered they can generate validation internally through audience size alone. Once you hit a certain threshold of followers, brands approach you. Media outlets interview you. Other influencers collaborate with you. Each of these interactions generates more visibility, which generates more followers, which generates more opportunities, and suddenly you're being treated as an expert without ever having to demonstrate expertise through any mechanism except the original accumulation of attention. The feedback loop operates independently of competence. You can be catastrophically wrong about everything, nutrition, investing, relationships, skincare, productivity, mental health, and as long as you maintain engagement, the system rewards you identically to someone who's actually correct. There's no penalty for wrongness as long as wrongness entertains.

The Parasocial Credibility Transfer

Instagram and TikTok engineered something television never achieved: the illusion of a direct relationship at scale. When someone appears in your feed daily, speaking directly to the camera in their bedroom or car, using casual language and acknowledging their "community," your brain processes this as a social connection. The parasocial relationship, one-sided emotional investment in a media figure, isn't new, but social media has weaponized it. Previous generations felt connected to television personalities or radio hosts, but those figures maintained professional distance. They performed in studios, spoke through scripts, and appeared as polished personas. The influencer aesthetic does the opposite: it's deliberately casual, allegedly unfiltered, designed to feel like friendship. You see them making breakfast, complaining about bad days, showing their kids or pets, or having messy apartments. The performance is so effective that audiences forget it's curated.

This manufactured intimacy transfers into unearned credibility. When someone feels like your friend, you extend trust that hasn't been earned through demonstrated knowledge or a reliable track record. They're not selling you something; they're recommending something to their friend, which happens to be you, along with three hundred thousand other "friends." The influencer who shares their morning routine can pivot seamlessly into promoting a supplement company, and their audience receives this as personal advice rather than paid advertisement, even when the post includes #ad hashtags required by FTC regulations. The hashtag satisfies legal requirements while doing nothing to disrupt the parasocial trust. Your brain still processes the recommendation as coming from someone who cares about your well-being, not someone executing a marketing contract designed to extract money from your wallet while giving you nothing beyond a temporary belief that you're making sophisticated health choices.

The economics here explain why this model proliferates. Traditional advertising required companies to produce content, commercials, print ads, and sponsorships, which were expensive and obviously promotional. Influencer marketing outsources content production to people who've already built audiences, costs a fraction of traditional campaigns, and comes wrapped in the authenticity aesthetic that makes it far more persuasive than anything that looks like advertising. A skincare company can pay fifty influencers to create personalized content about their product for less than a single television commercial and get better conversion rates because audiences trust influencers more than they trust advertisements. The influencer isn't even necessarily lying; they might genuinely like the product, or at least like the five thousand dollars enough to convince themselves they like the product. But whether they like it is irrelevant to whether it works, and audiences can't tell the difference between "this person got paid to say this" and "this person independently evaluated this and found it valuable." The system counts on that confusion.

Credential Simulation and Aesthetic Expertise

Watch how influencers in technical domains construct authority without possessing underlying knowledge. The finance influencer films content in front of a wall of leather-bound books they've never read, wears expensive watches, and uses terminology like "liquidity," "volatility," and "market corrections" without explaining what these terms mean or when they apply. The aesthetic signals expertise, the books, the business attire, and the confident delivery, while the content remains deliberately vague. They'll say things like "the market's looking uncertain, so it's important to diversify your portfolio and stay informed," which sounds knowledgeable but commits to nothing. It's financial horoscope language: broad enough to seem applicable regardless of what happens, specific enough to sound analytical.

Fitness influencers perfect this simulation differently. They have visible abs, which audiences interpret as evidence that they know how to generate visible abs in others. But personal results don't transfer into teaching ability, and genetic advantages don't translate into replicable methods. The influencer with perfect genetics and four hours daily for exercise can achieve results through almost any program, then sell that program to people with normal genetics and forty-five minutes three times weekly, and when it doesn't work, blame the customer for insufficient commitment. The aesthetic of fitness, the body, the gym setting, the athletic clothing, the sweat-drenched post-workout photo, substitutes for actual knowledge about exercise science, nutrition, recovery, or program design. They look like they know, which is enough.

The nutrition space demonstrates this pattern most dangerously. Someone eliminates gluten and feels better, maybe because they actually have celiac disease, maybe because eliminating gluten meant eliminating most processed foods, maybe because the placebo effect is powerful, and parleys this personal experience into a platform where they instruct thousands of people to eliminate gluten. They're not lying about their experience. But they're BSing about causation, about generalizability, about whether their singular anecdote constitutes evidence for anyone else. They film content in aesthetically pleasing kitchens, use terms like "gut health" and "inflammation" without explaining mechanisms, show before-and-after photos that might be separated by six years and perfect lighting rather than six months and dietary intervention. The aesthetic of wellness, farmers' market vegetables, mason jar smoothies, yoga poses at sunrise, signals expertise so effectively that audiences don't notice the absence of actual nutritional knowledge, understanding of metabolism, or ability to distinguish correlation from causation.

The Content Treadmill and Quality Degradation

Influencers face a structural problem: platforms reward frequent posting, but producing quality content takes time. The algorithm privileges accounts that post daily or multiple times daily. Miss a few days and your engagement plummets because the platform's distribution system deprioritizes dormant accounts. This creates impossible math. To maintain algorithmic favor, you need constant content, but to create content worth consuming, you need research time, editing time, and verification time. The solution every major influencer discovers is to lower quality standards until content production becomes sustainable. Instead of researching topics thoroughly, they react to trending topics with hot takes. Instead of investigating whether something works, they report that it worked for them. Instead of checking facts, they assume facts based on something they half-remember reading somewhere.

This quality degradation isn't visible to audiences because they rarely see the counterfactual, what the influencer could have produced with adequate research time. They see polished videos and assume effort, not realizing that production polish and content quality are independent variables. You can film in 4K, edit with professional software, add motion graphics and licensed music, and still be completely wrong about everything you're saying. The aesthetic polish makes wrongness look authoritative. An influencer can claim "studies show" without citing which studies or whether those studies were replicated or whether they're misrepresenting the findings, and most audiences won't check. Why would they? The production looks professional, the person seems confident, and verifying claims takes work that watching content doesn't.

The treadmill accelerates over time. Early in an influencer's career, they might spend a week researching a video. As their audience grows and platform demands increase, research time contracts to a day, then hours, then minutes. Eventually, they're just repackaging things other influencers said, creating a circular citation network where everyone's repeating everyone else, and nobody's checking primary sources. Someone makes up a statistic, "studies show 80% of success comes from mindset", and it spreads through influencer networks until it becomes an accepted fact despite no studies showing this because the statistic is meaningless. What studies? What definition of success? What measurement of mindset? The claim is unfalsifiable, which makes it perfect for the engagement economy. It sounds profound, requires no evidence, and audiences share it because it confirms what they want to believe about the importance of attitude over circumstance.

Manufactured Relatability and Strategic Vulnerability

The most sophisticated influencers discovered that appearing perfect generates admiration but not engagement, while appearing perfectly imperfect generates both. So they engineer vulnerability moments, posts about struggling with anxiety, videos about business failures, stories about relationship difficulties, but these confessions are carefully calibrated. The struggle is never so severe that it makes them seem incompetent, and it always resolves in ways that reinforce their expertise. "I almost quit my business last year, but then I discovered these three mindset shifts that changed everything" isn't vulnerability: it's a sales pitch using the aesthetic of vulnerability. Real struggle doesn't come with a three-point framework and a link to a course in the bio.

This manufactured relatability serves multiple functions. It makes the influencer seem humble and self-aware, which increases trust. It provides narrative tension that keeps audiences engaged. It positions failures as learning experiences that validate their current success, rather than as indicators that maybe they don't know what they're doing. And most importantly, it creates the impression that their success is replicable; they struggled just like you, but they figured it out, which means you can too, assuming you follow their advice and purchase their products. The vulnerability is strategic. They're not sharing their actual doubts, fears, or continuing struggles with problems that remain unsolved. They're sharing the sanitized version where every confession leads to triumph and every moment of weakness becomes a teaching opportunity.

The audience's participation in this dynamic reveals something uncomfortable about what we actually want from influencers. We claim we want authenticity, but authentic people don't post constantly, don't have perfect lighting, and don't turn every life experience into content. Actual authenticity is boring and inconsistent; people who are genuinely themselves have days where they're not insightful, moments where they're petty or lazy or uncertain. We don't want to watch that. We want the performance of authenticity: just enough "realness" to feel relatable, combined with just enough aspiration to feel worth following. We want them to seem like us but better, similar enough that their success seems achievable, different enough that their success seems worth envying. The influencer who threads this needle perfectly gives us what we want: the comfortable fiction that personal transformation is just a mindset shift and a morning routine away.

The infrastructure supporting influencer culture has adapted to make this performance frictionless. Photography apps include filters labeled "authentic" and "natural" that still adjust lighting and smooth skin, just less obviously than beautification filters. Content scheduling tools let influencers batch-produce authenticity weeks in advance. Engagement pods, groups of influencers who agree to like and comment on each other's posts, manufacture the appearance of organic community support. The entire ecosystem is designed to make performance look effortless and calculations look spontaneous. What the audience sees is someone living their best life and generously sharing insights. What's actually happening is professional image management by people who've figured out that appearing authentic is more profitable than being genuine, and considerably easier to maintain at scale.

The Expertise Marketplace and Manufactured Credentials

The influencer economy created a parallel credentialing system that operates independently of traditional gatekeepers. You don't need a degree in nutrition; you need before-and-after photos. You don't need a finance background; you need screenshots of your brokerage account. You don't need therapy training; you need to have "done the work" on yourself. This alternative credentialing system looks democratic until you examine what it actually validates. It credentials salesmanship, not knowledge. Photogenic results, not replicable methods. The ability to monetize attention, not the ability to generate outcomes for anyone except yourself.

The most telling evidence appears when influencers diversify. The fitness influencer launches a course on productivity. The productivity influencer releases a dating advice program. The dating coach starts selling financial education. There's no principle limiting their claimed expertise except market demand. If audiences will buy it, they'll teach it. Traditional credentialing systems, however flawed, at least imposed some subject-matter boundaries. A cardiologist doesn't typically moonlight as a corporate strategy consultant. A CPA doesn't usually offer couples therapy. The credentials meant something about domain focus. But influencer credentials mean something about audience capture, which applies across any domain where people experience dissatisfaction and can be sold the promise of transformation.

Watch the language they use when expanding into new territories. They don't claim expertise; they claim "passion" or "journey." "I've been on this financial freedom journey and wanted to share what I've learned." This phrasing does important work. It positions them as fellow travelers rather than experts, which insulates them from accountability when their advice fails. If you're an expert and your students don't get results, that's your failure. If you're just sharing your journey and your followers don't get the same results, well, everyone's journey is different. The framing is defensive by design, creating plausible deniability while still extracting expert-level pricing. The $2,000 course might be positioned as "investment in yourself" and taught by someone who positions themselves as "passionate about helping others." Still, the economic transaction is identical to hiring a consultant, except the consultant might actually have relevant expertise and professional liability.

The credential marketplace extends beyond individual influencers into an entire ecosystem of mutual validation. Influencers interview each other on podcasts, creating the appearance of peer review without any actual evaluation of competence. They collaborate on products, speak at each other's events, and write testimonials for each other's programs. This network functions like an academic citation, but without the scrutiny. When a researcher cites another researcher's work, that citation can be evaluated to determine whether the source was represented accurately. Is the source credible? Are there contradicting studies they ignored? When an influencer features another influencer, the audience sees endorsement from someone they trust, but there's no mechanism to evaluate whether that trust is warranted. The entire network could be mutually reinforcing incompetence, and from inside the ecosystem, it would look identical to legitimate expertise being properly validated.

The Crisis of Scale and Outsourced Authenticity

As influencer operations scale beyond individual capacity, they face a problem that reveals the fundamental fraud of the parasocial relationship. The audience believes they're connecting with a person. The influencer is actually a small media company. Behind the single face and first-person voice is a team: content producers, video editors, social media managers, engagement specialists, and administrative assistants. The DMs the audience thinks they're sending to their favorite influencer are read and answered by a twenty-two-year-old hired through a virtual assistant marketplace who's following scripts and decision trees for how to maintain the illusion of personal connection at scale.

Some influencers are transparent about this evolution. Most aren't. Transparency destroys the value proposition. If audiences understood they're interacting with a corporate entity rather than an accessible individual, the parasocial magic dissipates. So the machinery stays hidden. The influencer films content referring to decisions "I" made, using "my" singular voice, while a team of six people handles everything except appearing on camera. Some don't even handle that; they hire body doubles for certain types of content, use voice actors for podcasts when they're busy, and employ ghostwriters for books published under their name. The personal brand becomes entirely detached from any particular person but maintains the aesthetic of individual authenticity because that's what the audience pays for.

This creates a strange ontological category: a corporation that presents as a human, speaking with human intimacy about human struggles while operating with corporate structure and scale. The influencer posts about vulnerability and connection while their team implements A/B testing on emotional keywords to optimize engagement rates. They share "raw, unfiltered moments" that were reviewed by four people before posting. They build a "community" that's actually a customer acquisition funnel with friendship aesthetics. The dissonance doesn't trouble them because they've convinced themselves that the ends justify the means. If the content helps people, does it matter that it's more manufactured than it appears? This logic conveniently ignores that the help is often illusory and the manufacturing is exactly what makes it illusory.

Algorithmic Capture and the Death of Artistic Risk

The ultimate tragedy of influencer culture isn't the scams or the incompetence, it's what happens to people who actually have something valuable to share. The algorithm doesn't distinguish between substance and simulation. It rewards frequency, consistency, and adherence to proven formats. An expert with genuinely useful knowledge faces a choice: adapt to platform demands and degrade their content into algorithm-friendly fragments or maintain quality standards and accept algorithmic irrelevance. Most choose adaptation. The researcher who could produce one comprehensive, rigorous video monthly instead produces fifteen short-form reactions to trending topics because that's what the platform distributes. The artist who wants to create challenging work instead produces comfortable content that won't make anyone scroll past. The teacher who could genuinely educate becomes an entertainer who keeps people watching.

This isn't censorship, it's economic pressure that produces identical results. The platform doesn't forbid long-form, challenging, educational content. It just doesn't distribute it. And if your rent depends on distribution, you optimize for distribution. Over time, even people who started with integrity find themselves making compromises. Just this once, they'll make the thumbnail more clickbaity. Just this time, they'll simplify a complex topic into a misleading soundbite. Just for this video, they'll claim certainty about something they're actually uncertain about because nuance doesn't perform. Each compromise makes the next easier, until they can't remember what they were trying to say before the algorithm trained them how to speak.

The cost of this capture extends beyond individual corruption. It means the platforms selecting for information flow have systematically optimized for the wrong metrics, and everyone participating in the ecosystem gradually becomes shaped by those metrics. We don't get the best thinkers rising to prominence; we get the people most willing to adapt thinking into entertainment. We don't get the most accurate information spreading; we get the most engaging information spreading, and accuracy is at best uncorrelated with engagement, at worst inversely correlated because comfortable lies engage better than uncomfortable truths. The influencer economy doesn't just permit BS. It's structurally designed to make BS outcompete honest expertise and then reward the BSters with enough money and status that they can hire the actual experts to work for them. At the same time, they maintain control of the audience relationship. The face speaks. The brain remains hidden. And nobody watching knows the difference.

Chapter 7: The Wellness Industry: Selling Illusions of Health

The wellness industry has accomplished something remarkable: it's convinced millions of people that illness prevention requires continuous purchasing. Not one-time education. Not structural changes to food systems or labor conditions. Not healthcare reform. Purchasing. Monthly subscriptions to supplements that your body will excrete unchanged. Apps that gamify breathing. Retreats that promise cellular regeneration through expensive silence. The industry generated $1.5 trillion globally in 2023, and almost none of it correlates with measurable health improvements in populations that consume it most avidly. This isn't healthcare. It's the monetization of anxiety about a body you'll never perfect and a lifespan you can't actually extend through purchasing behavior.

What makes wellness BS distinct from other forms we've examined is its fusion of three volatile elements: pseudo-scientific language that sounds medical without being verifiable, the aestheticization of health as visible thinness or muscular definition, and the moralization of consumption choices as expressions of self-care. You're not just buying a $47 bottle of ashwagandha extract; you're investing in yourself, honoring your body, choosing wellness over sickness. The transaction gets framed as virtue rather than commerce, which makes questioning it feel like attacking someone's right to health rather than examining whether the product does anything at all. And because wellness operates in the murky space between functional medicine and outright quackery, it exploits regulatory gaps that allow marketers to make implications without claims, suggestions without evidence, promises structured carefully to avoid FDA scrutiny while still extracting belief.

The Biomarker Obsession and Quantified Self Delusion

Somewhere in the past decade, wellness culture became convinced that optimal health requires constant measurement. Not occasional checkups with actual physicians, but daily tracking of metrics most doctors consider clinically irrelevant for people without specific conditions. Your glucose levels after every meal are monitored through continuous glucose monitors marketed to non-diabetics. Your heart rate variability each morning is interpreted through algorithms that translate normal variation into warnings about stress. Your sleep cycles are measured through wearables that claim to detect REM stages despite lacking the equipment that sleep labs use. The tracking generates data, the data creates anxiety, and the anxiety generates purchases, supplements to optimize the numbers, apps to interpret the trends, consultations with health coaches who have no medical training but absolute confidence in their ability to read your biomarkers like tarot cards.

The continuous glucose monitor provides the perfect case study. These devices, originally developed for people with diabetes who need real-time glucose monitoring to avoid life-threatening events, now get marketed to metabolically healthy people as tools for "optimizing metabolic health." Companies like Levels and Nutrisense sell CGMs alongside apps that score your meals based on glucose response, creating a framework where eating an apple generates a graph, and the graph gets interpreted as data about your cellular health. The problem? Glucose naturally fluctuates throughout the day in response to countless factors, such as stress, sleep, exercise timing, hormonal cycles, and even the order in which you eat foods during a meal. These fluctuations are normal, not pathological. But the app doesn't tell you that. It treats every spike as a problem to solve, every variation as evidence that you need to modify behavior, purchase their recommended supplements, or upgrade to premium coaching.

The scientific literature on glucose variability in non-diabetic populations remains remarkably thin. Researchers know high average glucose correlates with diabetes and cardiovascular disease, but whether the specific fluctuations these monitors detect in healthy people predict any negative outcomes remains unproven. Nevertheless, wellness companies have built entire business models around the assumption that flatter glucose curves equal better health, and they've convinced consumers to pay $400 monthly memberships to chase that flattening. What gets sold as "data-driven health optimization" is actually behavioral manipulation through measurement, creating anxiety about normal physiology, then selling the solution to problems you didn't have until you started measuring.

The same pattern repeats across the quantified self landscape. Heart rate variability gets marketed as a stress metric, despite HRV varying wildly based on factors like caffeine intake, room temperature, and whether you measured before or after checking your phone. Sleep tracking apps claim to detect sleep stages using wrist movement and heart rate, despite research showing these devices misclassify sleep stages up to 40% of the time compared to polysomnography. None of this stops wellness companies from using the data to sell sleep supplements, meditation app subscriptions, or consultations with sleep coaches who will confidently diagnose your sleep dysfunction based on a wrist accelerometer's best guess about whether you were in REM.

The Supplement Industrial Complex and Epistemic Loopholes

Walk into any health food store, and you encounter shelves stacked with bottles making carefully calibrated promises.

"Supports immune function." "Promotes healthy inflammation response." "May help maintain focus." These phrases sound medical while committing to nothing verifiable. They exploit a regulatory structure created by the Dietary Supplement Health and Education Act of 1994, which allows supplement manufacturers to make "structure-function claims", statements about how ingredients affect body structure or function, without proving those claims through clinical trials. As long as they avoid claiming to treat, prevent, or cure specific diseases, and include the disclaimer "The Food and Drug Administration has not evaluated this statement," they can market products making health suggestions without demonstrating that those suggestions correspond to reality.

The result is an industry operating in a verification vacuum. Pharmaceutical companies must prove their products work through randomized controlled trials before marketing them. Supplement companies face no such requirement. They can sell products containing ingredients studied once in a petri dish, never tested in humans, extrapolated wildly from that single study into marketing language suggesting human health benefits, and face no regulatory consequences unless someone gets acutely poisoned. The burden of proof runs backward; supplements are assumed safe and effective until proven otherwise, rather than required to demonstrate safety and efficacy before sale.

Consider collagen supplements, which generated $4.7 billion in sales last year despite minimal evidence that they deliver advertised benefits. The marketing promises wrinkle reduction, joint health, and stronger hair and nails. The biological reality? Collagen is a protein. When you consume it, digestive enzymes break it down into amino acids, which your body uses for whatever it needs, not necessarily rebuilding the collagen in your skin or joints. Some studies show modest effects on skin elasticity, but the research remains sparse, industry-funded, and plagued by small sample sizes. More importantly, you could get the same amino acids from a chicken breast for a fraction of the cost. But chicken breasts don't come in Instagram-ready packaging with promises about "beauty from within," so they generate no premium pricing.

The magnesium supplement market reveals another layer of the con. Wellness influencers claim most people are magnesium-deficient and need supplementation for energy, sleep, anxiety, muscle function, and roughly fifteen other complaints. The medical reality? Clinical magnesium deficiency is rare in people eating varied diets, and the symptoms of actual deficiency are severe enough that they'd send you to a doctor, not to Whole Foods. But magnesium has become a wellness culture obsession, with dozens of companies selling various forms, magnesium glycinate for sleep, magnesium threonate for cognition, magnesium citrate for digestion, each marketed with the implication that choosing the wrong form means missing out on specific benefits. No robust evidence supports these form-specific claims, but the differentiation allows companies to sell multiple products where one would suffice, and to convince consumers they need expertise to navigate magnesium selection, expertise conveniently available through $200 consultations with nutritionists who learned about magnesium forms from the same wellness blogs as everyone else.

Detox Mythology and the Profitable Fiction of Toxin Accumulation

The wellness industry has convinced a substantial portion of the population that their bodies are warehouses of accumulated toxins requiring periodic purging through juice cleanses, infrared saunas, activated charcoal, or ionic footbaths that allegedly draw toxins out through the feet. None of these interventions removes toxins, because the entire premise misunderstands human physiology. Your liver and kidneys already detoxify continuously. That's their function. They don't need assistance from celery juice or a $300 sauna session. The toxins wellness marketers reference remain conveniently vague, "environmental toxins," "heavy metals," "metabolic waste", because naming specific compounds would require proving accumulation and demonstrating removal, neither of which these products can do.

Juice cleanses provide the template for detox BS. Companies sell three-day, five-day, or week-long protocols involving consuming only fruit and vegetable juices, claiming this gives your digestive system a "rest" while flooding your body with nutrients and eliminating toxins. The biological reality? Your digestive system doesn't need rest; it's designed to process food continuously. Juice removes fiber, which means you're getting sugar water with vitamins while eliminating the component of fruits and vegetables that actually supports digestive health and blood sugar regulation. You'll lose weight during a juice cleanse because you're consuming 800 calories daily instead of your normal intake, but the weight loss is water and glycogen, not fat or toxins. Within days of resuming normal eating, the weight returns. No toxins were eliminated. No organs were cleansed. You paid $300 to be hungry for a week while companies profited from your misunderstanding of metabolism.

The ionic footbath scam operates through even more transparent deception. You put your feet in a tub of water, a device runs an electrical current through it, and the water turns brown, orange, or green. Wellness practitioners claim the color represents toxins leaving your body through your feet. Run the same device with water but no feet, and the water changes color identically; the discoloration comes from electrode corrosion, not your toxins. The companies selling these devices know this. They sell them anyway, banking on consumers not running the control experiment, which requires skepticism and scientific thinking rather than the desperate hope that complex health problems have simple purchased solutions.

Activated charcoal represents detox BS in capsule form. Emergency rooms use activated charcoal for acute poisoning, which binds to certain substances in the stomach and prevents absorption. Wellness companies took that narrow medical application and extrapolated it into a daily supplement claiming to "cleanse" your system by binding toxins. But daily charcoal use doesn't selectively bind toxins while leaving nutrients alone. It binds whatever it encounters, which means it can reduce the absorption of medications and nutrients if taken regularly. The emergency room protocol involves single large doses in specific contexts, not daily supplementation. Nevertheless, activated charcoal appears in supplements, face masks, toothpaste, and expensive juices, all marketed with detox language that implies your body accumulates poison that needs regular purging.

The Guru Economy and Manufactured Chronic Illness

Wellness culture has generated a new professional category: the health guru who turns personal illness narrative into a business model. The pattern is consistent enough to constitute a genre. Someone experiences mysterious symptoms, fatigue, brain fog, digestive issues, and pain that conventional medicine fails to resolve satisfactorily. They begin experimenting with diet changes, supplements, and alternative therapies. They experience improvement, which may result from the intervention, from natural symptom fluctuation, from placebo effects, or from resolution that would have happened regardless. They attribute the improvement to their protocol, begin sharing it online, gather an audience of people with similar symptoms, and monetize that audience through supplements, courses, coaching, or books detailing their recovery.

The problem isn't that these people are lying about their experience; most genuinely believe they discovered what healed them. The problem is the leap from "this worked for me" to "this will work for you" to "I understand the mechanisms of chronic illness" to "I can teach you to heal yourself." That progression requires no medical education, no understanding of research methodology, no acknowledgment of individual variation, and no recognition that correlation doesn't equal causation. It just needs confidence and an audience.

Medical Medium, a brand built entirely on a man who claims to receive health information from a spirit, exemplifies how far this can go. Anthony William has no medical training, no scientific credentials, and no evidence beyond his own assertions that spirits feed him information about disease and healing. He's published several bestselling books, built a massive social media following, and convinced thousands of people to follow elaborate protocols involving celery juice, heavy metal detox smoothies, and supplement regimens. His recommendations contradict established science regularly. He claims viruses cause autoimmune diseases while asserting autoantibodies don't exist, claims the Epstein-Barr virus causes dozens of conditions despite no research supporting these connections, and sells supplement protocols costing hundreds monthly with zero evidence they work. None of this stops people from following his advice religiously, because wellness culture has taught them to trust personal testimony and spiritual authority over medical consensus.

The chronic Lyme disease community provides another example of how wellness entrepreneurs manufacture ongoing illness requiring ongoing payment. Chronic Lyme, as diagnosed by alternative medicine practitioners, differs dramatically from the medically recognized post-treatment Lyme disease syndrome. Alternative practitioners claim Lyme bacteria persist despite antibiotic treatment, causing virtually any symptom imaginable, and require years of expensive alternative therapies to eradicate them. Mainstream medicine finds no evidence for chronic Lyme as these practitioners describe it; tests come back negative, symptoms don't match Lyme disease presentation, and prolonged antibiotic protocols cause serious harm without benefit. But wellness practitioners created a diagnosis that explains medically unexplained symptoms, built treatment protocols that generate revenue, and fostered online communities that reinforce the diagnosis. Patients who might have recovered naturally or benefited from addressing underlying psychiatric or autoimmune conditions instead spend years and tens of thousands of dollars chasing an illness that exists primarily in the alternative medicine economy.

Biochemical Individuality as Unfalsifiable Marketing

The newest iteration of wellness BS wraps itself in the language of personalization. "Everyone's body is different." "What works for one person might not work for another." "You need to find what's right for YOUR unique biochemistry." These statements are technically true, individual variation exists, but they're wielded to make wellness protocols unfalsifiable. If someone follows a wellness guru's protocol and improves, the protocol works. If someone follows the same protocol and doesn't improve, they simply need to find what works for their unique biochemistry, perhaps a different guru's protocol, or the same guru's premium personalized consultation.

The functional medicine model perfects this approach. Functional medicine practitioners position themselves as investigating root causes while conventional medicine treats symptoms. They order extensive lab panels, dozens of tests measuring hormones, nutrients, inflammatory markers, gut bacteria, and interpret the results through frameworks that treat any value outside a narrow optimal range as pathological. They find "imbalances" that need correcting through supplements, dietary changes, and lifestyle modifications. The patient receives a binder full of test results and a treatment plan costing hundreds or thousands of dollars monthly.

The genius of this model is that it always finds something to treat. Lab values in human populations follow normal distributions; by definition, some percentage will fall outside average ranges without indicating disease. Functional medicine reframes this statistical reality as subclinical pathology requiring intervention. Your vitamin D is 28 ng/mL instead of the "optimal" 50 ng/mL they decided on? You need supplementation. Your cortisol pattern doesn't match their preferred curve? You have adrenal dysfunction needing adaptogenic herbs. Your gut bacteria composition differs from their template? You need probiotics, prebiotics, and an elimination diet to restore balance.

None of these interventions undergo rigorous testing to demonstrate that they improve outcomes. They're not treating diseases with known natural histories and measurable endpoints. They're treating lab abnormalities that may or may not cause symptoms, using protocols that may or may not change those labs, in patients who may or may not have been sick in the first place. When someone reports feeling better, the practitioner takes credit. When someone doesn't improve, the issue is that their biochemistry requires more investigation, more testing, more personalized intervention, which means more appointments and more revenue.

The appeal is obvious. Conventional medicine often fails patients with complex chronic symptoms. Doctors constrained by insurance limitations and appointment times may not investigate thoroughly or may default to psychiatric explanations when biomarkers look normal. Functional medicine offers time, attention, investigation, and the promise that your symptoms have physical causes that can be corrected. But offering attention doesn't make the interventions valid, and finding lab abnormalities doesn't mean those abnormalities caused your symptoms or that correcting them will resolve your problems. It just means someone paid attention and found something to bill for.

The metabolic typing approach takes personalization even further into unfalsifiability. Practitioners claim people fall into distinct metabolic types, fast oxidizers, slow oxidizers, protein types, carb types, each requiring specific macronutrient ratios for optimal health. They determine your type through questionnaires about symptoms and food preferences, then prescribe eating patterns allegedly suited to your metabolism. If you follow the recommendations and feel better, your kind was correctly identified. If you feel worse, either your type was misidentified and needs retesting, or you're experiencing "healing reactions" as your body adjusts, or your kind shifted and needs reassessment. The framework generates infinite opportunities for consultation and course correction, while remaining immune to disproof because any outcome can be interpreted as consistent with the model.

What all these personalization frameworks share is the exploitation of legitimate complexity to sell the illusion of precision. Human metabolism is extraordinarily complex, influenced by genetics, microbiome composition, sleep patterns, stress, exercise, medication, and countless other factors. This complexity means we can't make precise predictions about how specific individuals will respond to interventions. Wellness entrepreneurs take this legitimate uncertainty and claim they can navigate it, not through careful research, but through their proprietary frameworks, their intuitive assessments, and their ability to interpret your unique biochemistry. They're selling confidence about complexity, precision in uncertainty, and the promise that health optimization is just a $3000 protocol away. And because outcomes in wellness are subjective, delayed, and influenced by placebo effects, these entrepreneurs can maintain their businesses for years without ever demonstrating that their methods work better than doing nothing.

Chapter 8: Corporate Spin: The CEO's Toolkit of Deception

The quarterly earnings call operates like a séance where executives summon numbers from the spirit world and interpret them for believers. Revenue missed projections by twelve percent, but leadership describes this as "normalizing growth patterns in line with strategic repositioning." A product line hemorrhaging money becomes "an investment in future market penetration." Mass layoffs transform into "organizational optimization" or "rightsizing for efficiency gains." The language isn't designed to clarify; it's engineered to create a parallel reality where failure wears the costume of strategic thinking and disaster gets reframed as controlled evolution. What makes corporate BS particularly sophisticated is its self-contained ecosystem: companies control the metrics they're judged by the narratives explaining those metrics, the analysts asking questions about the narratives, and often the media reporting on the entire performance. It's not lying if you've constructed the whole measurement apparatus to make your version of events unfalsifiable.

The CEO who master's this toolkit doesn't need to deceive directly. The system does it for them through a combination of GAAP accounting flexibility, selective disclosure requirements, and a financial media apparatus that treats quarterly guidance like prophecy rather than guesswork.

When a company "beats earnings expectations," those expectations were set by the company's own forecasts, revised quarterly based on how the business was actually performing. Missing your own lowered guidance still counts as missing, but beating guidance you deliberately set conservatively gets celebrated as outperformance. The game is rigged at the level of scorekeeping itself.

The EBITDA Shell Game and Creative Definition

Stand in any investor conference and listen to executives tout their "adjusted EBITDA", earnings before interest, taxes, depreciation, and amortization. Already, this metric strips out costs that are, in fact, real costs the company must pay. But adjusted EBITDA goes further, removing whatever expenses the company decides aren't "recurring" or "core to operations." A company can lose money by every traditional measure while reporting positive adjusted EBITDA by defining away the losses. Restructuring charges? Non-recurring, exclude them. Legal settlements? One-time events, strip them out. Stock-based compensation that dilutes shareholders? Not a cash expense, ignore it. The marketing of merchandise that didn't sell? Not core to the business model.

WeWork provides the canonical case study, though they're hardly alone. The company reported "community-adjusted EBITDA," which excluded not just standard items but also basic operating costs like building renovations and preopening expenses for new locations. These costs were entirely predictable and central to their business model of leasing buildings, renovating them, and subleasing desk space. By this metric, WeWork was profitable. By the metric that includes money you actually spend running your business, they were incinerating cash. When your company is called "We", but the metric is adjusted to remove "work," you've achieved peak corporate BS.

The technique proliferates because it works. Analysts build financial models using whatever metrics companies provide, and if everyone in an industry reports adjusted EBITDA, that becomes the standard for comparison. Reporters write headlines about "earnings beats" based on adjusted figures because that's what moves markets, and market movement is news. Investors who dig into actual cash flows rather than adjusted metrics get dismissed as pessimists who don't understand the "unit economics" or "path to profitability." The company's definition of success becomes the only definition that matters, and anyone pointing out that the definition was reverse engineered to guarantee success gets accused of missing the bigger picture.

The Strategic Pivot and Retroactive Vision

Watch what happens when a company's core business fails. The language doesn't acknowledge failure; it announces vision. Executives who spent years promising dominance in market A suddenly reveal they were always building toward market B, and everything that looked like flailing was actually strategic experimentation. The narrative retrofit is so seamless that investors who lost money on market A start believing they're early adopters of market B's inevitable success.

Microsoft spent the early 2010s insisting mobile computing was its future, acquiring Nokia for $7.4 billion and pushing Windows Phone as the third ecosystem alongside iOS and Android. When this failed catastrophically, Windows Phone peaked at 3.4 percent global market share before collapsing, the company didn't announce defeat. CEO Satya Nadella reframed the entire history as the necessary groundwork for their real vision: cloud computing and enterprise services. The mobile disaster became "learnings" that positioned Microsoft for cloud dominance, even though its Azure cloud platform had nothing to do with phone operating systems. Investors who'd watched billions incinerate in mobile were convinced they'd actually witnessed strategic brilliance they'd been too shortsighted to recognize. The stock quintupled.

The mechanism here operates through temporal manipulation. Present failure gets recontextualized as a past strategy for future success. The CEO who can't make today's business work claims prescience about tomorrow's opportunity, and because tomorrow hasn't arrived yet, the claim remains unfalsifiable. You can judge whether Windows

Phone failed, but you can't yet judge whether that failure was "necessary" for cloud success because cloud success is still unfolding. By the time enough years pass to evaluate the claim, leadership has turned over, the narrative has calcified into company legend, and newer failures need reframing through newer visions.

Every tech company losing money tells some version of this story: they're not failing to build a sustainable business, they're "investing in growth" or "prioritizing market share over profitability." Amazon pioneered this excuse in the 1990s and actually made it work, running losses for years before achieving genuine profitability. Now every company burning cash invokes Amazon as proof that today's red ink becomes tomorrow's dominance. What they omit: Amazon was building real infrastructure, warehouses, logistics networks, and technology systems that created durable advantages. Most companies spending more than they earn are buying growth that evaporates the moment they stop spending, the equivalent of using investor money to pay customers to use a product that those customers don't value enough to pay for themselves.

The Manufactured Crisis and Executive Heroism

Corporate leadership has perfected a particular performance: discovering a crisis they created, announcing it dramatically, and then solving it through tough decisions that require lavish compensation for their courage. The CEO takes the stage and reveals that the company faces existential threats, competition is fiercer than anticipated, market conditions have shifted, and the previous strategy isn't working. What they don't mention: they designed the last plan, hired the team executing it, made the acquisitions that aren't working, set the targets they're now missing. The crisis isn't external weather; it's internal decisions compounding into disaster. But by framing it as discovered rather than caused, the CEO positions themselves as the solution rather than the problem.

The playbook follows predictable beats. First, acknowledge the severity to establish credibility: "We're not where we need to be," or "the numbers speak for themselves." Second, accept abstract responsibility while avoiding specific accountability, "leadership owns these results" without identifying which leader made which decision that led to which outcome. Third, announce the turnaround plan with enough detail to sound substantive but enough vagueness to avoid measurable commitments. Fourth, execute layoffs framed as "difficult but necessary decisions" that demonstrate toughness. Fifth, wait two quarters for comparisons against the previous disaster to show improvement, declare the turnaround successful, and collect a bonus for "extraordinary leadership during challenging times."

IBM has performed this cycle repeatedly over the past two decades. CEO after CEO inherits a company whose revenue has been declining for years, announces the decline is unacceptable and demonstrates urgency for change, restructures the business through layoffs and asset sales, maintains the illusion of stabilization for a few years through accounting maneuvers and cost-cutting, then departs to praise for their "steady hand" while leaving the next CEO to discover that revenue is still declining and another turnaround is needed. Ginni Rometty ran this exact playbook from 2012 to 2020, presiding over a 25 percent revenue decline while collecting $164 million in total compensation. Her successor, Arvind Krishna, immediately announced that IBM needed a dramatic transformation to reverse its trajectory, the same trajectory Rometty was supposedly transforming throughout her tenure.

The manufactured crisis creates permission for actions that would otherwise seem like failure. Layoffs aren't admissions that you hired too many people or managed them poorly; they're tough choices that demonstrate fiscal responsibility. Selling business units isn't acknowledgment that you overpaid for acquisitions or couldn't integrate them; it's "portfolio optimization" and "focus on core strengths." Slashing R&D budgets isn't mortgaging the future to make today's numbers; it's "improving operational efficiency." The language transforms every retreat into advance, every failure into opportunity, every forced decision into strategic choice.

The Acquisition as Narrative Reset

When organic growth stalls, companies acquire it, or more precisely, develop the story of it. The press release announcing the deal projects "synergies," "complementary capabilities," and "accelerated innovation." The acquiring CEO explains how this "transformative" combination creates a stronger competitor positioned for long-term success. Analysts build models showing how revenue from both companies, plus optimistic assumptions about cross-selling, equals growth. The stock price reacts to the narrative rather than operational reality, which won't become visible for years, by which time the executive who made the deal might have moved on. The acquisition's failure gets buried in broader business results.

Most acquisitions destroy value. Study after study shows that roughly 70 to 90 percent of acquisitions fail to deliver their promised benefits, they don't achieve projected synergies, they distract management, they create cultural incompatibility, and they overpay for assets that deteriorate post-purchase. Yet companies continue acquiring because the narrative value exceeds the operational reality. An acquisition lets leadership tell a story about growth and vision that's more persuasive than admitting their core business has matured or their strategy isn't working. It resets the clock on investor expectations, gives us three years to integrate this acquisition before judging results, and provides excuses if results disappoint, since integration is "complex" and "takes time."

Google's acquisition history illustrates how narrative value justifies operational waste. The company has purchased over 200 companies, many for hundreds of millions or billions of dollars, and then shuttered most of their products within a few years. Motorola Mobility: acquired for $12.5 billion, sold for $2.9 billion after eighteen months. Nest: acquired for $3.2 billion, products were discontinued or merged into other divisions that already existed. Fitbit: acquired for $2.1 billion, layoffs announced within two years. Each acquisition announcement projected strategic rationale, hardware capabilities, patent portfolios, and talent acquisition. The consistent failure suggests the real strategy is maintaining the appearance of innovation and growth through purchasing rather than building, knowing that a few small successes will be remembered. At the same time, dozens of expensive disasters get forgotten.

The language of acquisition announcements deserves its own taxonomy of BS. "Strategic fit" means we couldn't build this ourselves. "Synergies" means we plan to fire people and pretend the layoffs create value. "Complementary product lines" means we're hoping customers who buy A will buy B, though we have no evidence that this happens. "Enhanced innovation capabilities" means we're buying engineers because we can't recruit them. "Accelerated time to market" means our own development was failing. Every phrase translates from aspiration to admission once you learn the code.

The Purpose-Washing and Values Theater

Corporate leadership discovered that claiming to care about things beyond profit generates permission to continue pursuing profit without scrutiny. The technique is purpose-washing: wrapping conventional business operations in the language of social mission, environmental sustainability, or stakeholder capitalism while changing nothing substantive about how the business extracts value. It's more sophisticated than greenwashing, which focuses narrowly on ecological claims. Purpose-washing encompasses the entire spectrum of virtue, diversity, equity, sustainability, community, and purpose, translating each into corporate initiatives that satisfy no one except the marketing department.

Every major bank now publishes detailed ESG reports, environmental, social, governance, that enumerate their commitments to sustainability and social justice. These same banks continue financing fossil fuel extraction, providing mortgages with discriminatory impacts, fighting regulation that would limit predatory lending, and paying their executives several hundred times their median worker's salary. The reports exist to demonstrate concern, not to constrain behavior. They're compliance theater for stakeholders who might otherwise demand actual change, providing enough documentation to claim progress while preserving the business model that creates the problems being documented.

Unilever's "Sustainable Living Plan" exemplifies the genre. The company committed to halving its environmental footprint while doubling sales, improving the health and well-being of a billion people, and enhancing the livelihoods of millions. The plan generated extensive media praise for corporate responsibility leadership. The environmental footprint improved marginally through efficiency gains that also reduced costs. The health claims rested on selling soap and toothpaste in developing countries and counting users rather than measuring health outcomes—the livelihood enhancement involved supply chain standards that were difficult to verify and rarely enforced. Meanwhile, Unilever's core business remained manufacturing consumer products in disposable packaging using supply chains that extract natural resources at unsustainable rates. The plan lets them market their purpose while continuing business as usual.

The performance reaches its apex in CEO letters to shareholders that spend more words on stakeholder capitalism and long-term value creation than on the actual financial results or strategic decisions. These letters have become exercises in abstraction, paragraphs about "our commitment to our people" and "building a better future" that say nothing about layoff decisions or wage policies, claims about "environmental stewardship" from companies whose business models depend on resource extraction or energy consumption, promises of "diversity and inclusion" from leadership teams that remain overwhelmingly male and white. The language signals values while insulating those values from anything resembling measurement or accountability.

The Guidance Game and Expectations Management

The quarterly earnings cycle operates through a peculiar ritual: companies provide "guidance" about their expected performance, analysts adjust their estimates based on this guidance, and then everyone celebrates when the company "beats" expectations they effectively set themselves. This isn't forecasting, it's narrative construction with a three-month horizon. Companies that consistently beat expectations aren't superior at prediction; they're exceptional at managing the prediction game, setting bars low enough to clear while maintaining the appearance of ambitious targets.

Watch how guidance evolves through a quarter. Early guidance might be optimistic to maintain the stock price. Mid-quarter, companies with access to real-time sales data can see whether they're tracking to that guidance. If they're falling short, executives start preparing the market through "updated guidance" that lowers expectations while explaining the revision through external factors, macroeconomic headwinds, foreign exchange fluctuations, and timing of deals that were always unpredictable. By the time earnings are announced, estimates have adjusted downward enough that meeting the revised guidance counts as success, even though the company is performing worse than originally projected.

Companies that beat expectations consistently aren't magical; they're conservative in their guidance. Executives who know their business will generate $1.10 per share in earnings, provide guidance of $1.00, ensuring they beat by ten cents and get rewarded for outperformance. The obvious question, why not just offer accurate guidance?, has an obvious answer: beating expectations moves stock prices more than meeting them, even when "beating" means performing slightly better than your own sandbagged forecast. The market rewards the performance of exceeding expectations more than the reality of results themselves.

The sophistication comes in calibrating the lowball. Too conservative, and investors accuse you of managing expectations, treating guidance as artificial. The sweet spot is guidance that seems ambitious, slightly above the previous quarter, in line with long-term targets, but actually leaves room for the company to beat by a modest margin that seems like outperformance rather than sandbagging. This requires knowing your business well enough to forecast accurately, then deliberately shaving the forecast to create a beatable target. It's the opposite of honesty but gets rewarded as superior leadership.

The entire apparatus of analyst relations exists to facilitate this game. Companies host earnings calls with scripted remarks and selected questions, pre-brief analysts they want to influence, provide "investor materials" that highlight flattering metrics while burying unflattering ones, and cultivate relationships with analysts at major banks who need access to management to do their jobs. Those analysts face pressure to maintain positive ratings, too many "sell" recommendations, and the company restricts access, too many "buy" recommendations on companies that decline, and investors lose trust. The equilibrium is mostly "bought" or "hold" ratings, with occasional downgrades that are more theater than conviction, and price targets that drift with stock prices rather than drive them.

This system creates a self-reinforcing loop where corporate BS generates analyst BS generates media BS generates investor BS, all orbiting around companies that've learned to manage the perception of performance more effectively than performance itself. The quarterly earnings beat becomes the primary measure of success in a system that was supposedly designed to hold companies accountable to shareholders. Instead, it's become a mechanism for management to extract compensation by hitting targets they control, using metrics they define, against expectations they manage, while avoiding any accountability for long-term value creation that might require sacrifice today for payoff tomorrow.

The CEO's toolkit of deception isn't a collection of individual techniques; it's an entire grammar of corporate speech where every admission of failure gets conjugated into the future tense of strategic positioning, every present-tense disaster becomes past-tense learning that enables coming success, and numbers exist not to represent reality but to be interpreted through frameworks that make reality irrelevant. The executive who master's this language can preside over years of value destruction while collecting rewards for leadership, because the system measures what gets said about performance more carefully than it measures performance itself. That's not a bug in capitalism; it's capitalism discovering that controlling the narrative around value creation is easier and more profitable than actually creating value.

Chapter 9: Self-Delusion: The Lies We Tell Ourselves

The BS we consume from others is optional. We can turn off the television, unfollow the influencer, and skip the corporate memo. But the BS we generate internally, the stories we tell ourselves about who we are, what we're capable of, why things happened the way they did, operates without an off switch. It runs continuously in the background, shaping every decision, justifying every failure, protecting every comfortable delusion. We are our own most persuasive BS artists. Unlike external manipulators who need our attention to succeed, our internal narratives have a captive audience of one who never stops listening. The psychological mechanisms that allow us to maintain contradictory beliefs, rewrite our own histories, and construct flattering fictions about our motivations aren't bugs in human cognition; they're features that evolution selected for because they kept us functional in social environments where harsh self-assessment could be paralyzing. But what kept us functional in tribal environments now keeps us trapped in patterns we claim to want to escape. We say we value growth while avoiding every opportunity for it. We declare commitment to change while sabotaging the conditions that would make change possible. And most remarkably, we believe ourselves while doing it.

The Narrative Immunity System

Your brain operates a defensive perimeter more sophisticated than any nation's border security. Call it the narrative immunity system: a set of cognitive processes dedicated to protecting your self-concept from information that threatens it. When evidence arrives suggesting you're not as competent, ethical, or self-aware as you believe, this system deploys countermeasures without conscious instruction. The evidence gets reinterpreted, the messenger gets discredited, the context gets reconstructed until the threatening information either supports your existing self-image or disappears entirely. A performance review highlighting areas for improvement becomes evidence that your manager doesn't understand your role. A relationship ending because of your behavior becomes proof that you're better off without someone who couldn't appreciate you. A project failing due to your mistakes becomes a lesson about the importance of better team support. The original information, you need to improve, your behavior was destructive, your execution was inadequate, and it never penetrated the perimeter. It gets metabolized into something that reinforces rather than challenges your self-perception.

The mechanism operates through what researchers call motivated reasoning: the process by which we arrive at conclusions we want to reach by controlling which evidence we attend to and how we interpret it. But "motivated reasoning" sounds too deliberate, too conscious. What actually happens is more automatic. Your brain doesn't sit down and think, "I'd rather not believe this uncomfortable truth, so I'll find reasons to dismiss it." Instead, when you encounter information that conflicts with your self-image, your cognitive processes automatically generate arguments against that information while simultaneously failing to generate counterarguments. The skepticism feels natural, not motivated. You're not choosing to reject the evidence; you're recognizing its obvious flaws. The performance review really is poorly written. Your ex-partner really does have their own issues. The project really did lack adequate resources. None of these defensive observations is necessarily false. That's what makes the narrative immunity system so effective: it doesn't need to invent complete fictions. It just needs to emphasize the aspects of reality that support your preferred interpretation while conveniently overlooking the elements that don't.

Consider how this operates in professional contexts where you received clear feedback about deficiencies. A colleague tells you that you interrupt people in meetings, dominate conversations, and don't leave space for others to contribute. This is specific, actionable feedback about observable behavior. But watch what your narrative immunity system does with it. First response: identify a reason to discount the source. This colleague is conflict-averse, overly sensitive, and probably projecting their own insecurity about speaking up.

Second response: recontextualize the behavior. You interrupt because you're passionate and engaged. After all, meetings drag when no one drives the conversation, because your role requires decisiveness and leadership. Third response: generate counterevidence. Other colleagues haven't said anything, which proves this is one person's idiosyncratic interpretation rather than a pattern anyone else recognizes. Fourth response: reverse the moral valence. If anything, you should speak up more, not less, because organizations need people willing to move conversations forward rather than letting endless deliberation prevent action. By the time your narrative immunity system finishes processing this feedback, you've transformed a valid criticism into confirmation that you're exactly the kind of decisive leader organizations need. The person who delivered the feedback has been reconceptualized as someone whose passivity prevents them from recognizing valuable contributions. You haven't consciously lied to yourself. You've just allowed automatic cognitive processes to reconstruct reality until it stopped threatening your self-image.

The Retrospective Revision Engine

Memory isn't playback, it's reconstruction. Every time you recall an event, you're not accessing a stored recording but rebuilding the experience from fragments, filling gaps with inferences, and smoothing inconsistencies into a coherent narrative. This process operates silently and usually serves us well, allowing efficient information retrieval without perfect fidelity to the original experience. But it also means your past is continuously being rewritten to align with your present self-concept. The person you were five years ago gets updated to be more consistent with the person you believe you are now. Decisions you made for embarrassing reasons get retroactively re-motivated with better justifications. Relationships that ended badly get reframed until your role shifts from villain to victim or from passive participant to active agent of necessary change. You're not deliberately falsifying history; you're allowing your memory reconstruction process to operate with a thumb on the scale, weighing interpretations that preserve self-esteem while minimizing those that complicate it.

The retrospective revision engine runs most powerfully on decisions you can no longer reverse. The job you left, the relationship you ended, the opportunity you declined, these become subject to continuous reinterpretation because you can't test your revised narratives against alternative outcomes. You left that company because they didn't value innovation, not because you struggled to deliver results in their structured environment. You ended that relationship because you'd outgrown it, not because maintaining it required work you weren't willing to do. You declined that opportunity because you were being strategic about your career path, not because you were afraid of failure in an unfamiliar domain. The revision serves psychological function: it maintains belief in your decision-making competence by ensuring past decisions appear wise in retrospect. But it prevents learning. If every outcome gets reinterpreted until your choices look optimal, you never develop better judgment because you never acknowledge that previous judgment was faulty.

The most insidious revisions involve moral self-assessment. You remember yourself as having been more honest, more courageous, more principled than you actually were in situations where those qualities were tested. That time you stayed silent when a colleague was being treated unfairly gets remembered as a complex situation were speaking up would have been counterproductive, not as moral cowardice. That time you lied to avoid consequences gets remembered as a white lie that spared unnecessary hurt, not as self-protective deception. That time you took credit for someone else's idea gets remembered as a collaborative contribution where ownership was genuinely ambiguous, not as theft. The revision doesn't happen all at once. It occurs gradually, through repeated recall, where each reconstruction shifts the details slightly toward a more flattering interpretation. After enough iterations, you genuinely remember events differently from how they occurred. You're not lying when you tell the story; you're reporting what you remember. The BS has been internalized so thoroughly that it has become an autobiography.

The Exceptional Self Fallacy

Ask people how they rank themselves on nearly any positive trait, such as intelligence, honesty, driving skill, sense of humor, and a majority will place themselves above average. This statistical impossibility reveals something beyond simple arrogance: we genuinely believe we're exceptions to patterns we recognize in others. You know most people overestimate their abilities, but you're correctly assessing yours. You know most people have blind spots, but you've identified yours and compensated for them. You know most people rationalize their behavior, but your explanations represent accurate self-understanding rather than defensive reconstruction. This isn't garden-variety hypocrisy; it's a structural inability to apply general principles about human psychology to your own case. The mechanisms you recognize operating in everyone around you feel absent from your own experience because you have direct access to your internal states while observing only others' external behavior, and internal expertise always feels more nuanced, better justified, and more responsive to context than external observation reveals.

The exceptional self fallacy operates most powerfully in domains where you've invested significant effort or identity. The entrepreneur who failed three times before a modest success story doesn't think "I got lucky with timing and had access to capital that others lack." They think, "I persevered through setbacks others would have quit after because I had a vision they couldn't see." The middle manager who advanced through a combination of political skill and risk-aversion doesn't think "I excelled at institutional navigation while avoiding situations that could reveal my limitations." They think, "I demonstrated leadership and strategic thinking that earned recognition." The parent whose children succeeded academically doesn't think, "I had resources to provide advantages, and children whose temperaments happened to align with school requirements." They think "I instilled values and provided support that allowed them to reach their potential." None of these interpretations is entirely false; they're just systematically biased toward agency over luck, skill over circumstance, and character over context. You genuinely worked hard, demonstrated capability, and provided good parenting. But so did people whose businesses failed, careers stalled, and children struggled. The difference often comes down to factors outside your control but acknowledging that would require accepting that your success doesn't prove your exceptionalism. So the narrative immunity system emphasizes the elements you controlled while minimizing the elements you didn't, until your life story reads like a testament to individual agency rather than a complex interaction between effort and circumstance.

This fallacy becomes particularly destructive when it shapes how you respond to failure. If success proves your exceptionalism, external factors must cause failure;

otherwise, it will contradict your self-assessment. The job application was rejected after multiple interviews, becoming evidence that they wanted an internal candidate all along, not that stronger applicants existed. The pitch that failed to secure funding becomes proof that investors in your region don't understand innovation, not that your business model had fundamental weaknesses. The argument you lost becomes a demonstration that the other person was unreasonable or unwilling to engage in good faith, not that your position had logical flaws. This external attribution for failure combines with internal attribution for success to create a pattern where you never actually learn from mistakes because you've defined mistakes as events caused by forces beyond your control. You remain exceptional in your own estimation regardless of outcomes, which means you never identify what you need to change. The entrepreneur fails three more times, the manager's career stalls at the same level, the parents' second child struggles in ways the first didn't, and in each case, the exceptional self remains intact while outcomes continue contradicting it.

The Intention-Action Gap and Its Fictional Bridges

You intend to exercise regularly, starting Monday. You plan to stop checking your phone during conversations, starting now. You intend to save more money, be more patient, call your parents more often, read instead of scrolling, and do the difficult work during peak cognitive hours instead of burning daylight on email. These intentions feel like commitments, like decisions you've made that will shape future behavior. But intention without implemented structure is just narrative, a story you tell yourself about who you're going to be that requires no action in the present beyond the telling. The gap between what you intend and what you do is where the most persistent self-delusion operates, because as long as you maintain the intention, you can tell yourself you're the kind of person who does these things even while continuously not doing them.

The fictional bridges we build across this gap are marvels of psychological engineering—the most common: the permanent "starting Monday" clause. You'll begin the difficult change next week, next month, after this busy period ends, once circumstances stabilize. The start date functions as a release valve, letting you maintain identity as someone who takes this seriously without requiring present action. Monday arrives, circumstances haven't actually changed, the intention gets renewed with a new start date, and the cycle continues indefinitely. You're not lying about wanting to change; you're lying about when the change will begin, pushing it into a perpetually receding future where it never threatens present behavior. The intention remains intact, your self-concept as someone committed to improvement remains intact, and nothing actually changes.

Another bridge: the catastrophic-thinking exception. You'd exercise today, but you're already tired. At the same time, exhaustion could lead to injury, which would prevent exercise for weeks, so the responsible choice is to skip today and start fresh tomorrow. You'd have the difficult conversation with your colleague, but emotions are high right now and having it in this state could make things worse, so the mature choice is to wait for a better moment that somehow never arrives. The catastrophic thinking generates an endless supply of reasons why today is uniquely unsuitable for the intended action, while tomorrow will be perfect. The logic feels sound in each case. You are tired, emotions are high, but the pattern reveals that you're not making situated judgments about optimal timing; you're running an algorithm that reliably produces "not now" regardless of inputs.

The most sophisticated bridge: substituting consumption for action. You intend to start a business, so you read books about entrepreneurship, listen to podcasts about founder stories, and attend networking events where people discuss startups. You plan to improve your writing, so you follow writing advice accounts, buy courses about narrative structure, and discuss the craft with other aspiring writers. The consumption feels like progress because you're doing something related to the goal and acquiring relevant knowledge. But consumption without production is just preparation that never ends. You're not becoming an entrepreneur by reading about entrepreneurship; you're becoming someone who reads about entrepreneurship. You're not becoming a writer by studying writing advice; you're becoming someone who studies writing advice. The consumption lets you identify with the goal while avoiding the actual difficulty of pursuing it. You get to call yourself an aspiring entrepreneur or aspiring writer, which carries some of the status of the real thing, without taking the risks or doing the work that separates aspiring from doing.

The Sunk Cost Sanctuary and the Status Quo Lock-In

Once you've invested significant time, money, or identity in a path, admitting that path was wrong requires acknowledging that the investment was wasted. This creates psychological pressure to continue, not because continuation makes sense, but because stopping would mean accepting loss. The degree program that's clearly not leading where you thought becomes something to finish because you're already two years in. The relationship that stopped working years ago becomes something to preserve because you've invested a decade. The business model that's demonstrably failing becomes something to pivot repeatedly rather than abandon because you've burned through your savings building it. The sunk cost sanctuary operates by transforming past investment into present justification: the more you've already sacrificed, the more reason you have to keep sacrificing, because otherwise all previous sacrifice means nothing.

Economists know sunk costs should be irrelevant to present decisions; what matters is future costs versus future benefits, not unrecoverable past expenditure. But humans aren't economists. We're storytellers, and stories need coherent arcs where effort leads to reward. Quitting violates narrative expectations. It means the story was about someone who wasted years on a mistake rather than someone who persevered toward a goal. So we stay in situations we'd never enter now if given the choice, imprisoned by investment we can't recover. The sanctuary protection operates through a simple mechanism: whenever you consider leaving, your narrative immunity system generates arguments emphasizing progress made and minimizing problems. Things are improving, you're turning a corner, you've learned what doesn't work, which means success is closer, and the hard part is over. These claims might be true, but more often, they're just resistance to the narrative disruption that quitting would cause.

The status quo lock-in works similarly, but without requiring previous investment, it just requires present comfort. Change involves risk, uncertainty, and the possibility of discovering that different isn't better. Staying means knowing what you're getting, even if what you're getting is suboptimal. So you stay in the job that bores you because the alternative might bore you and pay less. You stay in the city you've outgrown because moving means starting over socially. You stay in the mindset that no longer serves you because adopting a new one means admitting the old one was wrong. The lock-in operates through risk asymmetry: you can vividly imagine ways change could make things worse while struggling to imagine ways it could make them better. The risks of change feel concrete and immediate, while the benefits feel abstract and distant. Your narrative immunity system exploits this asymmetry by emphasizing every possible downside while minimizing every possible upside until staying put feels like the obviously rational choice, even when you explicitly claim to want change.

The combination of sunk cost sanctuary and status quo lock-in creates patterns where people spend decades in situations they'd advise their younger selves never to enter. The lawyer who hates practicing law but can't quit because of the investment in law school and the lifestyle that law firm income supports. The couple that should have separated years ago, but can't because of property, children, and the identity disruption divorce would cause. The person who's been "working on" the same creative project for a decade without progress, because admitting it's not working would mean accepting that ten years were spent on something that will never materialize. In each case, the person can articulate exactly why they're stuck; they're not delusional about the constraints. But they're delusional about whether those constraints are actually constraints or just narrative protections preventing the discomfort of change. The lawyer could retrain, take the income hit, and build a different life. The couple could separate, work through the logistics, and discover they're both happier apart. The stalled creative could abandon the dead project and start something new with what they've learned. The constraints aren't physical laws; they're psychological commitments to stories that feel too expensive to revise.

The Comparison, Manipulation, and Selective Benchmarking

You assess your success by choosing your comparison group, and you select comparison groups that make you look good. When evaluating your career, you don't compare yourself to the most successful people in your field; you compare yourself to the median, or to people who started with fewer advantages, or to your high school classmates who went into less prestigious careers. When evaluating your fitness, you don't compare yourself to people at the gym; you compare yourself to people your age who don't exercise at all. When evaluating your parenting, you don't compare yourself to people whose children are thriving across multiple domains; you compare yourself to parents whose children are struggling more than yours. The comparison manipulation isn't conscious fraud; it's automatic strategic positioning where you gravitate toward benchmarks that confirm you're doing well while avoiding benchmarks that would suggest otherwise.

The selective benchmarking serves two functions: it protects self-esteem, and it justifies not trying harder. If you're already above median, why push for excellence? If you're already better than your starting point suggested you'd be, why not be satisfied with that? If you're already doing better than specific others, what more is there to prove? The comparison group becomes a ceiling disguised as a floor. You tell yourself you're comparing to assess realistic progress, but you're actually comparing to establish that present performance is adequate. This wouldn't be problematic if you owned it, if you said, "I've decided to prioritize sustainability over excellence, so I'm satisfied with median performance." But you don't own it. You maintain aspirations toward excellence while manipulating comparisons to avoid confronting the gap between aspiration and reality.

The manipulation becomes particularly sophisticated when you use different comparison groups for other contexts. When discussing your achievements, you compare yourself to people who've accomplished less, emphasizing how far you've come. When excusing your limitations, you compare yourself to people who've accomplished more, highlighting how unrealistic their standards are. You're simultaneously above average when that serves self-esteem and disadvantaged by impossible standards when that excuses underperformance. The contradiction doesn't register because you're not running both comparisons simultaneously; you're deploying whichever comparison supports the narrative you need in each specific moment. This isn't strategic lying so much as opportunistic truth-selection, where you have a menu of accurate comparisons and you instinctively choose the one that makes you look best given present rhetorical needs.

The most destructive form of selective benchmarking involves comparing your internal experience to others' external presentation. You compare your anxiety, self-doubt, and private struggles to other people's curated confidence, published achievements, and public success. This guarantees unfavorable comparison because you're comparing your rough draft to their final product, your behind-the-scenes chaos to their polished performance. But instead of recognizing the asymmetry, you conclude that everyone else has it figured out while you're barely holding together. This comparison doesn't just damage self-esteem; it prevents you from recognizing that your internal experience is normal. Everyone else is also anxious, uncertain, and struggling. They just don't show it. But your narrative immunity system treats their external presentation as evidence of internal state while treating your internal state as evidence of your inadequacy. The resulting conclusion, that you're uniquely struggling while everyone else glides through life effortlessly, is pure BS, but it's BS that feels like objective observation because you actually are working and they actually do look confident. You just can't see that the relationship between internal state and external presentation is radically different from what you assume.

The cost of self-delusion isn't just that you believe false things about yourself. It's that false beliefs drive real decisions. You stay in situations that harm you because you've convinced yourself they're temporary or necessary. You avoid challenges that would help you grow because you've convinced yourself you're protecting against failure. You repeat patterns that don't work because you've convinced yourself each iteration is different. The narrative immunity system keeps you comfortable in the short term while ensuring long-term stagnation, and the tragedy is that you experience this stagnation as mysterious bad luck rather than a predictable consequence of systematic self-deception. You're not a victim of circumstance; you're a victim of your own BS. But admitting that would require the very self-awareness that self-delusion exists to prevent.

Chapter 10: Media Noise: The Role of Information Overload

The human brain evolved to process roughly one hundred and fifty meaningful social relationships, Dunbar's number, the cognitive limit on stable connections our ancestors maintained in tribal groups. That same brain now receives sixty-three thousand words of information daily across multiple platforms, from sources numbering in the thousands, about events occurring simultaneously across every continent. We're operating neural machinery designed for a village while trying to comprehend a planet. This mismatch doesn't produce confusion or paralysis. It makes something more dangerous: the illusion of understanding generated through exposure rather than comprehension. You scroll through two hundred headlines before breakfast and mistake that scrolling for knowledge acquisition. You've seen information about climate negotiations, currency fluctuations, parliamentary votes in countries you'll never visit, wars you can't locate on a map, and celebrity divorces presented with identical urgency. Your brain tags all of it as "processed" without distinguishing between what you've actually understood and what you've merely witnessed passing by. This isn't information consumption. It's information skimming elevated to a lifestyle, and it's created an environment where BS doesn't need to be convincing anymore; it just needs to be present, loud, and repeated until familiarity gets mistaken for truth.

The volume itself becomes the weapon. When a thousand sources emit contradictory claims simultaneously, verification stops being a practical option. You can't fact-check everything, so you default to tribal heuristics: belief follows affiliation. If sources your in-group trusts say X, you believe X, not because you've evaluated the evidence, but because sorting truth from fiction at scale exceeds human cognitive capacity. Media organizations understood this shift decades ago. They're no longer competing to be the most accurate source; they're competing to be the most present source, the one that captures attention through sheer ubiquity and emotional resonance. Fox News doesn't persuade viewers that its perspective is correct through superior argumentation. They persuade through constant presence, creating an information environment so total that alternative perspectives require active seeking rather than passive encounter. MSNBC operates identically from a different tribal position. The content differs, but the mechanism remains constant: dominate attention bandwidth until your framing becomes the default lens through which everything else gets interpreted.

The Velocity Problem and Retraction Asymmetry

Consider the mechanics of how false information moves compared to corrections. A study from MIT examining Twitter data found that false news spreads six times faster than accurate news, reaching fifteen hundred people six times quicker than true stories. The researchers controlled for bot activity; this wasn't automated manipulation but human choice. We prefer false news because it's novel, surprising, and emotionally arousing. Truth tends to be boring, confirming what we already suspected, failing to generate the outrage or shock that makes us hit share. A fabricated story about a politician eating immigrant children will reach millions before a correction clarifying that, no, actually, completely made up, reaches thousands. By the time reputable sources publish debunking articles, the false story has already formed impressions, shaped beliefs, and moved on to become "something I heard about" that lives in memory disconnected from its disproven status.

The retraction never catches the lie because media velocity rewards first-mover advantage regardless of accuracy. Publication speed matters more than verification rigor because audiences have moved on by the time you correct yesterday's story. Rolling Stone published an article about a gang rape at a University of Virginia fraternity, describing a horrific assault in graphic detail. The story was false, key facts didn't check out, the alleged victim's account contained contradictions, and the event likely never occurred. Rolling Stone retracted the article, published an external review excoriating their editorial process, and lost a defamation lawsuit. But the retraction reached a fraction of the people who read the original story. Years later, surveys still found substantial percentages of people believed the UVA gang rape happened as described, unaware the story had been thoroughly debunked. The impression persisted independent of correction because impressions form faster than facts, and once formed, they resist revision. Your brain doesn't want to expend the energy required to update its model of reality. It's easier to ignore the correction than to integrate new information that contradicts what you've already filed away as known.

Media organizations understand this asymmetry and exploit it systematically. They publish sensational stories with minimal verification, generating massive traffic and attention. When those stories fall apart under scrutiny, they issue corrections in tiny fonts, buried on interior pages or in the scroll-past sections of websites. The correction satisfies legal requirements without materially impacting the false belief they've already distributed. The New York Times published a story claiming U.S. intelligence agencies had agreed Russia hacked the Democratic National Committee to help Trump win the 2016 election, citing "seventeen intelligence agencies" as the source. This number got repeated across media for months, becoming a central talking point in arguments about election interference. The actual number was four agencies: the FBI, CIA, NSA, and Office of the Director of National Intelligence. The Coast Guard and the Defense Intelligence Agency, among others, had nothing to do with the assessment. The Times eventually corrected this, changing "seventeen agencies" to "four agencies" in the online version without acknowledging the error prominently. But "seventeen intelligence agencies" had already become part of the discourse, cited in congressional hearings and international news, living on in public memory despite being factually wrong. The correction couldn't unring the bell because by the time it arrived, the false number had already served its purpose: establishing the impression of overwhelming intelligence consensus through numerical magnitude.

The Attention Economy's Extractive Logic

Media companies stopped selling information and started selling attention. The shift seems subtle, but it inverts everything about how journalism functions. When revenue came primarily from subscriptions, newspapers needed to maintain subscriber trust over time. You canceled if they proved unreliable because you were paying for long-term value. That model created incentives for accuracy, not perfect incentives, but directional pressure toward getting things right. Digital advertising destroyed that alignment. Now revenue comes from eyeballs: page views, click-throughs, and time-on-site metrics that advertising exchanges pay for. The payment isn't conditional on whether the content was accurate, useful, or valuable. It's conditional only on whether someone looked at it long enough for the ad to load.

This change weaponized emotional manipulation. The content that generates the most page views isn't the most informative; it's the most emotionally arousing. Anger, fear, and outrage drive clicks more reliably than sober analysis. BuzzFeed's internal research revealed that content eliciting high-arousal emotions (rage, anxiety, amazement) generated four times the sharing behavior of low-arousal content (sadness, contentment, information). Media organizations optimized accordingly. Headlines became weapons designed to trigger emotional responses strong enough to overcome the friction of clicking. "Politician proposes tax reform" gets ignored. "Your taxes are about to EXPLODE under insane new plan" gets clicked, shared, and monetized, even if the content behind the headline is identical. The headline is the product. The article is just an excuse for showing you the headline.

Watch how this plays out during election cycles. Media coverage of polling data focuses obsessively on horse-race dynamics, who's up, who's down, momentum shifts measured day-to-day, because that framing generates perpetual novelty and emotional stakes. Coverage of actual policy positions receives a fraction of the attention because policy is static and complex, generating neither the novelty nor the emotional arousal that drives engagement. A Pew Research Center analysis found that in 2016, horse-race coverage accounted for 42% of all election news while policy coverage accounted for 10%. Voters consistently tell pollsters they want more policy information and less horse-race coverage. Media organizations consistently deliver the opposite because what audiences say they want and what they actually click on diverge dramatically. The attention economy rewards giving people what they'll compulsively consume, not what they claim to value.

The economic pressure creates a race to the bottom that individual organizations can't escape, even if they want to. A newspaper that decides to prioritize accuracy over speed will get beaten on every story by competitors who publish first and correct later. A news site that refuses to optimize headlines for emotional arousal will lose traffic to sites that do, watching their advertising revenue decline while competitors thrive. The market punishes restraint and rewards recklessness. This isn't a moral failing of individual journalists; it's structural pressure that makes thoughtful journalism economically nonviable at scale. ProPublica can do deep investigative work because nonprofit grants, not advertising, fund it. Small independent outlets can prioritize accuracy because they're not trying to compete with the engagement metrics of media giants. But mainstream media, trapped in the attention economy, can't afford to optimize for truth when survival requires optimizing for clicks.

Algorithmic Amplification and the Manufactured Consensus

Social media platforms introduced a mechanism that makes information overload not just prevalent but personally targeted. Facebook's News Feed algorithm doesn't show you a chronological list of posts from accounts you follow. It shows you what the algorithm predicts will keep you engaged, based on billions of data points about your past behavior and the behavior of users the system has identified as similar to you. Twitter's algorithmic timeline works identically. TikTok's "For You" page is entirely algorithmic; you never choose who to follow, the system decides what to show you based on watch time and interaction patterns. These algorithms don't optimize for truth, utility, or your stated preferences. They optimize for engagement, measured through proxy metrics like time spent, shares, comments, and clicks. The content that keeps you on the platform longest is the content you see, regardless of whether it's accurate, representative, or good for you.

Research by Guillaume Chaslot, a former YouTube engineer, revealed how recommendation algorithms create radicalization pipelines. He made dozens of YouTube accounts with innocuous starting points, someone interested in fitness, vegetarianism, or jogging, and let the autoplay recommendations run. Within hours, the accounts were being recommended conspiracy theories, extremist political content, and pseudoscience. Why? Because that content has higher watch time. Someone who clicks on a video about healthy eating might watch three minutes. Someone who clicks on a video claiming that governments are poisoning food supplies with chemtrails watches twelve minutes. The algorithm doesn't understand or care about content quality.

It only sees that conspiracy content has better engagement metrics, so it recommends more of it, creating feedback loops that pull users toward increasingly extreme material, not because they're predisposed to extremism but because the algorithm has learned that extremism is sticky.

This creates manufactured consensus through selective exposure. You don't see a representative sample of perspectives; you see the perspectives the algorithm has learned that will keep you engaged. If the algorithm detects that you engage more with content that makes you angry, it shows you more anger-inducing content. Your feed fills with outrage, and because feeds are the primary way most people encounter news and opinions, you start to believe that outrage is the dominant response to events. Everyone seems furious all the time because the algorithm has filtered your information environment to show you fury preferentially. Meanwhile, someone else with different engagement patterns sees a completely different information landscape, and neither of you realizes that you're experiencing algorithmically constructed realities rather than representative samples of what people actually think.

The platforms understand this dynamic and refuse to change it because engagement is revenue. Facebook conducted internal research showing that its algorithm amplified polarizing content and misinformation because polarizing content generated more engagement. The research was leaked by whistleblower Frances Haugen, revealing that Facebook knew its platform was causing social harm through algorithmic amplification but chose not to modify the algorithm because doing so would reduce engagement metrics. Mark Zuckerberg received these internal reports. He chose continued algorithmic amplification over reducing social harm because the business model requires it. YouTube likewise knows that its recommendation algorithm radicalizes users but resists fundamental changes because recommendation drives 70% of watch time. The platforms can't fix the problem without destroying their business model, so they issue statements about "taking concerns seriously" while changing nothing structural.

Information Collapse and the Impossibility of Shared Reality

The volume and velocity of contradictory information don't just make individual verification difficult; they destroy the possibility of a shared factual foundation. Consider COVID-19, an event significant enough that you'd expect eventual consensus about basic facts. Three years after the initial outbreak, substantial populations maintain contradictory beliefs about fundamental questions. Was it engineered in a lab or naturally occurring? Depends on who you ask, and both groups will cite scientists, studies, and government documents supporting their position. Are masks effective at reducing transmission? Some studies say yes, others say no, and the meta-analyses conflict. Should healthy people under fifty have been vaccinated? The medical establishment said yes, but excess mortality data in some age cohorts now suggest more complicated risk-benefit calculations, and disentangling vaccine effects from virus effects from lockdown effects from reporting changes exceeds the analytical capacity of most individuals and apparently many health agencies.

The problem isn't that truth doesn't exist; it's that the information environment contains enough contradictory expert testimony that truth becomes practically inaccessible to normal people with jobs and lives. A motivated individual could spend five hundred hours reading studies, evaluating methodology, checking funding sources, and examining data quality. They still wouldn't reach certainty because the experts themselves disagree, and judging which experts are correct requires technical knowledge that the motivated individual likely doesn't possess. So people default to trust networks: they believe the experts their tribe trusts, which means factual disagreement becomes tribal identity rather than evidence-based conclusion. You can't have productive policy debates when different factions operate from incompatible factual premises, and you can't reconcile factual premises when the information environment is too noisy for anyone to hear a signal through static.

This collapse enables BS to flourish because verification becomes both impossible and pointless. Why fact-check a claim when tomorrow brings two hundred new claims equally suspect? Why research a topic deeply when the depth reveals only more contradiction rather than resolution? The rational response to information overload isn't increased scrutiny, it's decreased scrutiny, because scrutiny costs time that could be spent on anything else. The payoff (slightly less uncertainty) doesn't justify the investment. We settle for tribal priors and surface plausibility. If something sounds like what our trusted sources would say, we accept it. If it contradicts tribal priors, we dismiss it. The information environment has become so polluted that this heuristic, terrible as it is, beats actually trying to evaluate truth value claim by claim. We've created conditions where BS and truth are functionally indistinguishable to most observers most of the time, not because people are stupid but because distinguishing them requires resources nobody has.

The media landscape adapted to this reality by abandoning even the pretense of objectivity. Why maintain neutrality when half your audience will hate you regardless of how carefully you report? Why restrain editorial voice when the audience is selecting sources based on tribal affiliation rather than accuracy? Fox and MSNBC don't compete for the same viewers; they compete to be the dominant voice within their tribal coalition. The business model shifted from "trusted general source" to "trusted tribal voice," which means success comes from confirming what your audience already believes while framing everything through their preferred ideological lens. You're not selling information. You're selling identity reinforcement, and the more noise fills the information environment, the more valuable that identity reinforcement becomes because it provides psychological shelter from the overwhelming chaos of contradictory claims.

We built an information ecosystem that produces BS faster than any human cognitive system can filter it. The volume overwhelms verification. The velocity rewards first-movers over accurate reporters. The algorithms amplify engagement over accuracy. The economic model rewards clicks over truth. And the result is an environment where BS doesn't need to be convincing; it just needs to be present, repeated, and aligned with tribal priors. The machinery runs automatically now, generating noise at volumes that make signal extraction impossible. We're drowning in information while starving for knowledge and mistaking the drowning for drinking.

Chapter 11: Spotting the BS: A Practical Guide

You can't protect yourself from BS you can't identify. And identification is harder than it looks because BS has evolved sophisticated camouflage. It doesn't announce itself. It wears the costume of expertise, sincerity, data-driven decision-making, or peer-reviewed legitimacy. The most dangerous forms have learned to pass every superficial test; they cite sources, use technical terminology, acknowledge complexity, and even include disclaimers that make them look more honest than they are. What you need isn't a list of red flags to memorize. You need a diagnostic framework that works across contexts, a set of pressure tests that expose structural weaknesses in claims regardless of domain. This chapter provides exactly that: practical techniques for detecting BS in real time, before it extracts money from your wallet, time from your calendar, or belief from your cognitive reserves.

The first thing to understand: spotting BS isn't about fact-checking every claim. That's impossible. You don't have time to verify whether the productivity guru actually doubled their output using their five-step system, or whether the supplement company's clinical trial was properly blinded, or whether the business book's success stories survived contact with reality. Factchecking is retrospective, labor-intensive, and assumes you already suspect something. What you need is prospective detection, the ability to recognize BS structures before investigating their contents. These structures operate consistently. A medical quack uses the same rhetorical architecture as a business consultant selling transformation, which uses the same architecture as a political operative selling reform. The domains differ, but the load-bearing deceptions remain identical. Learn to spot the architecture, and you can navigate any environment where BS competes for your attention.

The Certainty-Complexity Mismatch

The single most reliable indicator of BS is inverse correlation between claimed certainty and underlying complexity. When someone presents a simple, confident answer to a genuinely complicated question, you're witnessing either profound ignorance or calculated manipulation. Both produce identical output: confident wrongness delivered with enough conviction to bypass your skepticism. The nutritionist who tells you exactly which foods cause inflammation is BSing because inflammation pathways involve dozens of molecular mechanisms, hundreds of contributing factors, and massive individual variation. The financial advisor who guarantees returns in a specific range is BSing because markets incorporate millions of decisions by participants with conflicting information and objectives, operating in systems with feedback loops that make prediction fundamentally unreliable beyond gross generalizations. The leadership consultant who promises your company culture will transform in ninety days is BSing because organizational culture emerges from accumulated behaviors, embedded incentives, historical norms, power dynamics, and individual psychology across potentially thousands of people, none of which respond to ninety-day programs the way the consultant's slide deck suggests.

This mismatch operates as a filtering mechanism. When you encounter a claim, ask: "How complicated is the system this claim addresses?" Then ask: "How certain is the person making this claim?" If certainty exceeds what the system's complexity permits, you've found BS. A climate scientist saying, "global average temperatures will rise between 1.5 and 4.5 degrees Celsius by 2100, depending on emissions trajectories," is offering appropriate uncertainty for a system involving atmospheric physics, ocean dynamics, feedback loops, and human behavior. A politician saying "this policy will create exactly 500,000 jobs" is BSing because job creation involves business decisions, market conditions, technological changes, consumer behavior, and competitor responses, none of which can be predicted to the precision of three significant figures. The certainty-complexity mismatch doesn't just identify overconfidence. It identifies intentional deception dressed as expertise, because actual experts know the limits of their knowledge and communicate those limits. BS artists need you to believe they've transcended those limits.

Watch for what we might call "precision theater", the deployment of specific numbers to create the illusion of rigorous analysis behind vague conclusions. The consultant who says "our analysis shows you're leaving 23.7 percent of potential revenue on the table" wants you to notice that decimal point. It signals measurement, calculation, and scientific rigor. But ask what was measured, how it was calculated, what assumptions went into the model, and whether that precision survives reality-testing, and the number evaporates into motivated guesswork. The personal finance guru who claims their investment strategy delivers "consistent 12-15 percent annual returns" wants you to register those specific percentages as evidence they've discovered something reproducible. But ask about methodology, which years, which market conditions, whether the backtest includes transaction costs and taxes, how they handled dividends and rebalancing, and you'll find either no answers or answers that reveal the returns existed only in hypothetical portfolios that never faced real-world friction.

The Evidence Substitution Game

BS rarely operates without evidence. That would be too obvious. Instead, it substitutes weak evidence for strong evidence while presenting the substitution as equivalent. The key is recognizing evidence hierarchies, understanding that not all supporting information carries the same epistemic weight, and identifying when someone is passing off a lightweight data point as if it were a heavyweight proof. An anecdote is not the same as a case study. A case study is not the same as an observational study. An observational study is not the same as a randomized controlled trial. A single RCT is not the same as a meta-analysis of multiple RCTs. And none of this matters if the person citing the evidence misrepresents what it actually shows.

The most common substitution: replacing outcome data with process data. The business book that promises to teach you the habits of successful people doesn't provide evidence that adopting those habits causes success; it provides evidence that some successful people exhibit those habits. These are not the same thing. Correlation without a mechanism for causation is just pattern-matching, and humans are extraordinarily good at finding patterns in noise. The successful people might have succeeded despite those habits rather than because of them. Or those habits might be effects rather than causes; people who achieve success gain resources that make certain habits easier to maintain. The productivity system that claims "thousands of users report feeling more organized" is substituting self-reported perception for measured output. Do they actually complete more work? Miss fewer deadlines? Produce higher-quality results? Or do they just feel more organized while accomplishing the same amount? The feeling generates positive testimonials. The accomplishment is what you're actually buying the system to achieve. One is not evidence for the other.

Learn to distinguish between demonstrations and validations. A demonstration shows that something can work under specific conditions. A validation shows that something does work reliably across varied conditions. The diet program that presents before-and-after photos is offering demonstrations, proof that some people lost weight using this program. What's missing is validation: controlled comparison showing people using this program lose more weight than people not using it, maintained over time periods longer than the initial weight loss, accounting for dropout rates and selection effects. The photos tell you nothing about whether the program works better than any other intervention, including doing nothing. They tell you only that some subset of participants achieved visible results worth photographing. This is evidence, but it's the weakest possible form, selected success stories that could emerge from random chance if enough people try the program.

The research citation game provides another substitution vector. Someone makes a claim, then cites a study, creating the impression that the study supports the claim. But read the actual research and you'll often find it says something adjacent to, narrower than, or contradictory to what the citation claimed. The supplement company, citing "clinical research," might be referencing a study that found a biochemical effect in cell cultures, not humans. Or a study in humans that found statistical significance in a secondary outcome after testing forty different variables, which is what happens when you run enough tests on small samples. Or a study funded by the supplement company itself, conducted by researchers with financial stakes in positive findings, using cherry-picked participant selection criteria that ensured favorable results. The citation exists to discourage investigation. Most people won't click through to read the methodology section. They'll see "clinical research shows" and grant it authority that the research doesn't warrant.

The Unfalsifiable Pivot

Legitimate claims make themselves vulnerable to disproof. They specify conditions under which they would be wrong, they define terms precisely enough that you could test them, and they acknowledge limitations and boundary conditions. BS, by contrast, engineers itself to be unfalsifiable, structured so that no possible evidence could disprove it, which means no evidence actually supports it either. When you can't specify what would make a claim wrong, the claim isn't making contact with reality. It's floating free in rhetorical space, immune to verification.

Watch how this operates in practice. The career coach promises their program will help you "unlock your potential" and "discover your authentic purpose." What would disprove this? Suppose you complete the program and feel unchanged.

In that case, the coach can say you didn't implement the strategies correctly, or you weren't truly committed, or you're experiencing resistance that's actually part of the breakthrough process. If you feel changed but see no external results, the coach can say internal transformation precedes external manifestation, and you need to trust the process. If external results appear, those validate the program. If they don't, their absence becomes evidence that you need more coaching. The claim has been engineered so that every possible outcome supports it. This isn't just unfalsifiable; it's a perfect trap. You can't win because winning and losing have been defined such that both count as winning for the person making the claim.

The political version operates identically. The candidate promises to "fight for working families" and "restore common sense to government." What specific policies does this entail? What measurable outcomes would indicate success? What timeline are we evaluating? None of this gets specified because specification creates accountability. If the candidate promised to reduce unemployment to below 4 percent within two years through specific legislative actions, you could evaluate whether they delivered. But "fighting for working families" can mean anything from passing meaningful labor protections to simply continuing to say you're fighting for working families while doing nothing. The vagueness isn't accidental; it's the load-bearing pillar of the BS. Remove it and the claim collapses.

Test for falsifiability explicitly. When someone makes a claim, ask: "What evidence would prove this wrong?" If they can't answer, or if their answer includes escape routes ("Well, it depends on..." or "That would just mean we need to adjust the approach..."), you're dealing with BS. Legitimate expertise can specify failure conditions. The engineer who designs a bridge can tell you exactly what forces would cause it to collapse. The economist making a prediction can say to you what economic conditions would invalidate their forecast. The doctor recommending a treatment can specify what symptoms would indicate the treatment isn't working. If the person making claims about your life, career, health, or future can't determine what failure looks like, they're not offering expertise; they're offering a belief system designed to perpetuate itself regardless of results.

The Complexity Concealment Problem

BS doesn't just oversimplify; it actively conceals complexity in ways that make questioning seem ignorant. The person delivering the BS frames their simple answer as if acknowledging complications would be pedantic, academic, or evidence of overthinking. This is tactical. Real complexity threatens the BS's persuasiveness, so the BSter must make complexity itself seem like the problem rather than the acknowledgment of reality. The result is an environment where the person introducing nuance gets treated as if they're obscuring a simple truth rather than preventing a simple lie.

The real estate seminar provides the template. The speaker explains how "anyone can build wealth through real estate investing" using their seven-step system. Someone in the audience asks about market timing, interest rate sensitivity, vacancy risk, maintenance costs, or local zoning regulations. Watch what happens. The speaker doesn't engage the specifics. Instead, they pivot to frame the question as evidence of limiting beliefs or analysis paralysis. "That's exactly the kind of overthinking that keeps people stuck. Successful investors take action. They don't wait for perfect conditions." The message: complexity is your enemy, and simplicity is your friend. The reality: complexity is the actual reality, and simplicity is the speaker's sales pitch. The person asking about vacancy risk is introducing a real factor that affects real outcomes. The speaker deflecting from that factor is protecting a profitable fiction that only works if attendees don't think too hard about whether the system functions as advertised.

This pattern repeats across domains with remarkable consistency. The management consultant selling organizational transformation discourages questions about implementation barriers, cultural resistance, competing priorities, resource constraints, or historical attempts at similar changes. These complications threaten the transformation narrative, so they get reframed as "organizational antibodies" or "change resistance", problems to overcome rather than information about whether the proposed transformation is actually feasible. The alternative health practitioner selling a protocol for chronic illness deflects questions about conflicting studies, the mechanism of action, or alternative explanations for reported improvements. These complications threaten the protocol's appeal, so they get dismissed as "Western medicine's reductionist thinking" or "the limits of conventional research." The pattern: complexity concealment packaged as clarity, skepticism reframed as limitation.

Deploy the "explain it to an intelligent skeptic" test. When someone is selling you something, a product, service, ideology, or self-image, imagine explaining their claim to someone smart who has no stake in believing it. What questions would that skeptic ask? Can you answer those questions using the information the seller provided? If the seller's framework can't withstand basic skeptical inquiry without requiring you to first accept premises that beg the question, you're looking at BS. Legitimate expertise can survive intelligent skepticism because it's built on mechanisms that make contact with how things actually work. BS requires you to turn off your skepticism first, to accept that questioning is the real problem rather than being the solution.

The Consensus Fabrication

Humans are social creatures who use perceived consensus as a heuristic for truth. If many people believe something, we assume they know something we don't, or at minimum that the belief has survived some collective vetting process. BS exploits this shortcut ruthlessly by fabricating the appearance of consensus where none exists, or by inflating minimal consensus into universal agreement. The key is learning to distinguish between actual expert consensus, where people with relevant knowledge and no conflicts of interest converge on a conclusion after examining evidence, and manufactured consensus, where marketing creates the illusion of agreement through selective amplification and strategic omission.

Pay attention to how consensus gets claimed. "Experts agree" is different from "some experts believe" is distinct from "leading voices in the field suggest" is distinct from "research indicates." These phrases create different levels of evidentiary weight while often getting used interchangeably in ways that smuggle weak claims under the protection of strong language. The cryptocurrency promoter who says "financial experts agree that blockchain represents the future of money" is claiming expert consensus. But which experts? Academics who study monetary systems? Central bankers? Economists? Blockchain entrepreneurs with financial stakes in adoption? The composition matters enormously, and the vagueness of "financial experts" allows the promoter to gesture toward credibility without being specific enough for you to verify whether the claimed consensus exists.

The "nine out of ten dentists recommend" pattern has evolved. Modern BS doesn't make easily checked claims about surveyed professionals. Instead, it creates the impression of consensus through social proof mechanisms that are harder to verify but feel similarly authoritative. The online course claims "over 50,000 students" have enrolled, a number that suggests popularity and therefore value. But enrollment isn't completion. Completion isn't satisfaction. Satisfaction isn't actual learning or improved outcomes. The number conflates all these while representing none of them specifically. Similarly, the business framework touted by "Fortune 500 companies" might have been purchased by one division of three Fortune 500 companies for a pilot program that got quietly discontinued when it produced no measurable value. But "used by Fortune 500 companies" sounds like validation, and few buyers will investigate whether "used by" means "found valuable" or "bought and abandoned."

Check for consensus through dissent. Legitimate expert consensus exists when you can't easily find credible dissenting voices, not because they've been silenced, but because the evidence is strong enough that qualified experts converge on the same conclusion despite having no incentive to agree. Evolution. Climate change. Germ theory. The effectiveness of vaccines. These have a genuine expert consensus because the evidence is overwhelming and the methodology is sound. Manufactured consensus, by contrast, requires you not to look for dissenting experts, because finding them is trivially easy. The diet industry claims "experts agree" that their approach works, but nutritional science is famously divided, with qualified experts taking opposite positions on most questions about optimal diet. The productivity methodology claims "top performers" use their system, but successful people use contradictory systems, suggesting the system isn't the relevant variable. When consensus must be protected through selective amplification rather than surviving open inquiry, you're looking at fabrication.

The Temporal Displacement Trick

One of BS's most effective techniques is temporal displacement, locating promised benefits or demanded evidence in timeframes that make verification impossible or irrelevant. The mechanism works by creating enough distance between claim and verification that by the time reality could disprove the BS, either you've moved on, the BSter has moved on, or the context has changed enough that accountability dissolves. This isn't the same as making predictions that take time to validate. Legitimate long-term claims specify mechanisms, intermediate milestones, and falsification conditions. Temporal displacement simply pushes consequences beyond the horizon where accountability operates.

The classic version appears in retirement planning and long-term investment schemes. The financial product promises "wealth accumulation over 30-40 years" using projections that assume historical returns continue indefinitely, fees remain stable, markets don't crash during critical accumulation years, and you maintain contributions without interruption. These are enormous assumptions, but they're dressed in the costume of conservative planning because the timeframe is so long. By the time you discover whether the projections matched reality, decades have passed, the person who sold you the product has retired or changed careers, and the financial firm has restructured three times under different management. The temporal distance makes accountability impossible. You can't test the claim until it's too late to act on the information, and the seller faces no consequences for wrong projections because the causal chain connecting their recommendations to your outcomes has too many confounding variables.

Watch for claims that locate all meaningful results beyond your practical planning horizon while demanding immediate action or payment. The anti-aging supplement promises "longevity benefits that accumulate over years of use", benefits you won't be able to verify until you're old, at which point whether you lived to 85 or 87 will depend on so many factors that isolating the supplement's effect becomes impossible. The leadership development program promises "career transformation that unfolds over five to ten years", long enough that whether you got promoted has more to do with organizational restructuring, economic conditions, and luck than the program's curriculum, but packaged as if the program deserves credit for any positive career movement during that window. The environmental policy promises "measurable impact by 2050", distant enough that the politicians advocating for it won't be in office when the measurement happens, and far enough that interim failures can be explained away as implementation challenges rather than flawed assumptions.

The flip side of this technique: demanding immediate action before you have time to verify claims or consider alternatives. "Limited time offer," "enrollment closes Friday," "only three spots remaining", these artificial scarcity tactics create urgency that short-circuits deliberation. The pressure to act now prevents you from doing the research that would reveal the BS. The real estate seminar pushes you to sign up for the advanced coaching program before leaving the hotel, offering a "special rate" that disappears at midnight. The online course emphasizes that "doors close in 48 hours" and won't reopen for six months. The supplement company offers a "founding member discount" that expires before you have time to investigate whether their proprietary blend contains anything beyond what you could buy generically for a fraction of the cost. The temporal squeeze, buy now, verify later, operates as a defense mechanism for BS that can't survive scrutiny.

The diagnostic move: ask what happens if you wait. If the answer is "the opportunity disappears," ask whether that makes sense given what you're actually buying. Digital products have no scarcity; courses, eBooks, and software can be replicated infinitely at zero marginal cost. Physical products that aren't genuinely rare or seasonal have no reason to impose purchase deadlines except to prevent you from comparison shopping. Services from consultants, coaches, or advisors don't evaporate if you take a week to think, unless the consultant knows that thinking is their enemy. Whenever urgency appears arbitrary rather than inherent to what's being sold, you're looking at BS trying to bypass your defenses by collapsing the time you have to activate them.

The Credential Misdirection

Legitimate expertise is domain-specific and earned through demonstrated competence in that specific domain. BS artists know this, so they've developed sophisticated techniques for borrowing credibility from adjacent domains or creating the appearance of expertise through credentials that don't actually qualify them for the claims they're making. The result is a landscape where impressive-sounding credentials get deployed strategically to shut down skepticism without actually indicating relevant expertise. Your job is learning to evaluate whether credentials connect to competence in the specific area where claims are being made.

The most common pattern: leveraging credentials from one domain to establish authority in another. The physician who pivots from practicing medicine to selling business success systems wants you to transfer the authority medicine grants them into an entirely different domain where that authority doesn't apply. Medical training doesn't provide special insight into entrepreneurship, productivity systems, or wealth building. But "Dr." in front of a name creates a halo effect that makes people more likely to trust advice in any domain, even when the doctorate is irrelevant to the advice. Similarly, the former military officer selling leadership consulting wants you to transfer the authority of military service into corporate management, but tactical operations under life-or-death conditions have fundamentally different dynamics than quarterly planning cycles in organizations where the stakes are budgets and market share. The skills aren't transferable in the ways the consultant implies, but the credential does rhetorical work that makes questioning them seem disrespectful.

Watch for credential inflation through vague affiliations and carefully worded descriptions. "Harvard-trained" might mean they attended a two-day executive education seminar at

Harvard, not that they earned a degree there. "Published researcher" might mean they co-authored a single paper fifteen years ago in a field unrelated to their current claims. "Award-winning" might reference an award from an industry trade organization that gives awards to anyone who pays for membership. "Certified" might indicate they completed an online course from an organization they themselves created specifically to certify people in their proprietary methodology. None of these is technically false, but all of them develop impressions that exceed reality. The inflation is intentional; it's designed to make you think they've achieved more than they have, endured more scrutiny than they have, demonstrated more competence than they have.

Apply the specificity test. When someone deploys credentials, ask specific questions about what those credentials actually indicate. What did they study? Where did they conduct research? Who evaluated their work? What are their qualifications for the specific claim they're currently making? The nutritionist selling a gut health protocol might have a legitimate degree in nutrition, but did their training include the microbiome research they're now claiming expertise in, or are they extrapolating from basic nutrition knowledge plus selective reading of studies they're not qualified to interpret? The business consultant might have worked at McKinsey, but were they analyzing healthcare operations while now selling manufacturing optimization, meaning their experience doesn't transfer as cleanly as the

McKinsey credential implies? Credentials are data points, not trump cards. They tell you what someone studied or where they worked, not whether they're correct about the claim in front of you right now.

The ultimate test for BS isn't any single technique; it's the accumulation of defensive patterns. Legitimate expertise can withstand questioning, welcomes specificity, acknowledges limitations, and provides pathways to verification. BS requires you to accept vagueness, trust credentials without verification, dismiss complications as overthinking, and act before investigating. One defensive pattern might be circumstantial. Three or four together form a clear picture. The supplement company that makes vague claims, cites irrelevant research, fabricates consensus, and demands immediate purchase is BSing. The career coach who promises unfalsifiable transformation, conceals implementation complexity, manufactures urgency, and inflates credentials is BSing. Your job isn't to exhaustively investigate every claim. It's to recognize these patterns quickly enough to protect yourself from manipulation disguised as opportunity.

Chapter 12: Beyond the Fog: Seeking Truth in a World of Deception

Truth-seeking in 2024 isn't a virtue; it's a hobby for people with too much time and too little sense. The culture rewards speed over accuracy, confidence over verification, narrative coherence over factual precision. When a story breaks, the first person to tweet wins attention, the second person to confirm wins credibility, and the person who waits to verify gets accused of overthinking. By the time the actual investigation happens, the narrative has calcified into received wisdom, and anyone questioning it looks like a contrarian or a fool. This creates a peculiar dynamic: the people most committed to truth-seeking find themselves perpetually behind the information curve, always arriving after conclusions have been reached, always questioning what everyone else has already decided to believe. The fog doesn't just obscure truth; it creates structural incentives to stop looking for it. So what does it mean to seek truth when the environment punishes that seeking, when the mechanisms designed to surface truth have been captured by the very forces that benefit from obscuring it, when even our own cognitive architecture works against clear seeing? It means accepting that truth-seeking isn't about discovering capital-T Truth, some pristine fact untouched by interpretation, but about building better BS detectors and learning to live with perpetual uncertainty instead of fleeing into comfortable fictions.

The Economic Costs of Verification

Here's what nobody tells you about truth-seeking: it's expensive in ways that make it structurally disadvantaged against BS. BS is cheap. You can generate it in seconds. Verification takes hours, sometimes weeks, and often requires specialized knowledge or access to information deliberately kept scarce. When a celebrity doctor claims that a specific supplement protocol cured their autoimmune condition, debunking that requires understanding immunology, researching the supplement's actual mechanisms, reviewing clinical trial literature, evaluating the quality of that literature, understanding the publication bias in supplement research, and then translating all of that into accessible language. That's forty hours of work minimum. The original BS took thirty seconds to post and reached a million people before the verification even began. The economics don't just favor BS; they make truth-seeking a luxury good accessible only to people with resources and time. Journalists used to be paid to do this work, but most newsrooms gutted their investigative teams and replaced them with aggregators who rewrite press releases and summarize other outlets' reporting. The few remaining investigative reporters are spread so thin they can only tackle massive stories, the Pentagon Papers, not the wellness influencer making dubious health claims to a hundred thousand followers. Academic researchers could fill this gap, but their incentive structure rewards publishing in prestigious journals, not public education, and the knowledge they produce remains locked behind paywalls that make it inaccessible to the general public even when it's funded by taxpayer money. What emerges is a verification vacuum where BS propagates freely while truth-seeking becomes an act of unpaid labor performed by volunteers who get accused of having too much time on their hands.

Consider the information environment around COVID-19 vaccines, not the political battleground, but the actual epistemological challenge of determining what was true. A person trying to make an informed decision faced: preliminary research released as preprints before peer review, peer-reviewed studies with varying methodologies and quality, institutional guidance from CDC and WHO that updated as understanding evolved, pharmaceutical company press releases that cherry-picked favorable data, social media testimonials from people claiming various reactions, news coverage that sensationalized both benefits and risks, political figures making claims unsupported by evidence, and a scientific establishment that had lost public trust through decades of conflicts of interest and irreproducibility crises. Sorting through this required epidemiological literacy, statistical sophistication, understanding of immunology, ability to evaluate research methodology, awareness of institutional incentives, and probably two hundred hours of sustained attention. Meanwhile, anti-vaccine activists simplified everything into a coherent narrative:

pharmaceutical companies are corrupt, governments are authoritarian, natural immunity is superior, and the vaccine is dangerous. That narrative was false, but it was comprehensible and didn't require a graduate education to evaluate. The truth was complicated, uncertain, probabilistic, and required trusting institutions that had repeatedly betrayed that trust. The economic calculation was obvious: believing the simple story costs nothing, seeking the actual truth costs everything.

Epistemic Learned Helplessness and the Retreat to Tribalism

After enough encounters with fog, people stop trying to see through it. They develop what we might call epistemic learned helplessness, the conviction that truth is unknowable, that every source is biased, that reality itself is just competing narratives with no way to adjudicate between them. This isn't postmodern philosophy; it's a rational response to an information environment deliberately designed to exhaust verification capacity. When you discover that the industry funded the study, you read it exonerated, that the expert you trusted has undisclosed conflicts, that the news source you relied on ran a correction buried on page seventeen three weeks later, you start believing that everything is corrupt. There's no point trying to find solid ground. This belief is wrong, but it's understandable. The constant revelation of hidden agendas, manipulated data, and narrative management creates a kind of epistemological vertigo where nothing feels stable. People respond by retreating to tribalism, deciding that truth equals whatever my side says, and dismissing opposing claims not through evaluation but through pattern-matching to enemy territory. If the liberal media reports X, conservatives assume not-X by default. If the scientific establishment recommends Y, alternative health communities assume not-Y as the starting position. This isn't reasoning; it's using political affiliation as an epistemic shortcut, treating team loyalty as a proxy for truth-evaluation.

The mechanism operates through what researchers studying misinformation call "identity-protective cognition"; people process information in ways that protect their group identity rather than maximize accuracy. Show someone evidence that contradicts their political tribe's position, and their brain doesn't process it as information to evaluate; it processes it as a threat to social standing. Rejecting the evidence isn't about truth; it's about maintaining a connection to your community. This makes sense evolutionarily: for most of human history, getting expelled from your social group meant death, while being wrong about empirical facts had limited consequences. Natural selection optimized us for social survival, not objective truth-seeking. The problem is that modernity requires evaluating complex technical claims where tribal affiliation offers no guidance and getting things wrong has massive consequences. Whether ivermectin treats

COVID-19 isn't a question your political tribe can answer, but people treat it like one anyway because tribal thinking feels secure in ways that technical evaluation doesn't. The fog becomes comfortable; it lets you stop doing the impossible work of verification and just believe what your people think.

The Weaponization of Doubt and Strategic Uncertainty

The fossil fuel industry spent sixty years demonstrating that you don't need to establish falsehood; you just need to manufacture sufficient doubt that people stop trusting the truth. Internal Exxon documents from the 1970s show that their own scientists understood climate change, predicted its impacts with remarkable accuracy, and warned executives about the risks. The executives responded by funding think tanks and PR campaigns designed to convince the public that climate science was uncertain, that more research was needed before action, and that responsible people should remain skeptical of alarmist claims. This wasn't lying about the facts; it was creating an atmosphere of manufactured controversy where none existed scientifically. The strategy worked brilliantly. For decades, media outlets gave equal time to climate scientists and industry-funded skeptics, treating a scientific consensus as a he-said-she-said debate. The public internalized that the question remained open, that legitimate experts disagreed, that taking action would be premature until the science was "settled", a standard that's impossible to meet because science never reaches absolute certainty, only increasing confidence. By the time the manufactured doubt began to dissipate, thirty years had been lost.

This playbook gets deployed everywhere now. The tobacco industry pioneered it in the 1950s when research linking cigarettes to lung cancer emerged. Their response wasn't to deny the research, which would be too easily disproven, but to emphasize uncertainty, fund alternative studies that muddied the waters, and position themselves as advocates for more research before rushing to judgment. "Doubt is our product," one internal memo declared, "since it is the best means of competing with the 'body of fact' that exists in the minds of the general public." The pharmaceutical industry uses it when safety concerns emerge around profitable drugs: instead of defending the drug's safety directly, they emphasize the complexity of the question, the need for additional research, and the preliminary nature of warning signs. The sugar industry funded research in the 1960s designed to shift attention from sugar to fat as the dietary villain, successfully reorienting nutritional guidance for decades. Each sector learns from the others, refining techniques for strategic uncertainty, not eliminating truth, but making it so foggy that people give up trying to see clearly.

What makes this particularly pernicious is that the demand for certainty becomes a weapon against knowledge. Science operates through the gradual accumulation of evidence, increasing confidence that never reaches 100 percent. Any findings can be challenged as "not yet proven definitively," any consensus can be framed as premature, and any recommendation for action can be positioned as rushing ahead of the evidence. Climate deniers still use this strategy: they've largely stopped denying that warming is happening and pivoted to uncertainty about attribution (is it really human-caused?), magnitude (how much will temperatures rise?), impacts (will it really be that bad?), and solutions (will proposed interventions work without destroying the economy?). Each question creates another decade of manufactured controversy, another delay in action, another opportunity for fossil fuel extraction to continue. The person honestly seeking truth faces an impossible standard: they need perfect certainty before supporting action, while the status quo, which is also a choice, also has consequences, gets to operate under no evidentiary burden at all. The weaponization of doubt means that truth-seeking becomes an asymmetric battle where those defending reality must prove their case beyond all possible objections. At the same time, those spreading fog just need to keep asking questions.

Building Personal Verification Protocols

So what does truth-seeking look like when the environment actively opposes it? It starts with accepting that you cannot verify everything and must build triage systems for directing limited attention. Most claims you encounter don't matter enough to verify: someone's opinion about a TV show, speculation about a celebrity relationship, political hot takes that will be forgotten in a week. Spending cognitive resources on this material isn't truth-seeking; it's feeding the outrage machine. The claims worth verifying are the ones with consequences: information you'll use to make decisions that affect your health, finances, relationships, or understanding of how power operates. This requires developing a hierarchy of verification based on stakes. If someone recommends a restaurant, you don't need to research health inspection records; the worst case is a mediocre meal. If someone suggests a medical intervention, you need primary sources, not testimonials. If someone claims systemic fraud in elections, you need evidence strong enough to overcome the prior probability that systems designed by thousands of people over decades mostly work. Not every claim deserves equal skepticism. Extraordinary claims require extraordinary evidence; ordinary claims can accept ordinary proof.

The practical protocol looks something like this: First, identify the claim's source and its potential incentives. Is this person selling something? Do they benefit from you believing this? Does their identity or livelihood depend on this claim being true? Incentives don't make claims false, but they suggest where to focus skeptical attention. Second, check whether the claim is making empirical predictions or value judgments. "This supplement will boost your energy" is empirical and can be tested; "you should prioritize self-care" is a value statement that verification can't adjudicate. Don't waste time trying to fact-check values. Third, look for the strongest counterarguments against the claim. If you can't find any, you're in an echo chamber and need to search harder. People who actually know what they're talking about can articulate the strongest objections to their position; charlatans pretend no reasonable person could disagree. Fourth, trace claims back to primary sources. Did the news article about a study actually link to the survey? Does the study say what the article claims? Was it published in a reputable journal? What was the sample size? Who funded it? Have other researchers tried to replicate it? Fifth, accept that you'll often land in uncertainty rather than certainty, and that uncertainty is an answer. "The evidence is mixed and we genuinely don't know yet" is the truth, even though it feels unsatisfying compared to confident declarations from people who haven't done the work.

Developing Calibrated Skepticism

The truth-seeker's curse is that after you've discovered how often you've been deceived, every claim starts looking suspicious. You develop a hair-trigger BS detector that fires constantly, leaving you trapped in cynicism where nothing can be trusted and every institution is presumed corrupt. This is as dysfunctional as credulity, just in the opposite direction. The goal isn't maximum skepticism; it's calibrated skepticism that matches doubt to evidence. Some institutions are more trustworthy than others. Some sources have better track records. Some domains have more robust verification mechanisms. The National Weather Service forecast is generally reliable because weather prediction has good feedback loops; they make predictions, reality proves them right or wrong quickly, and errors get corrected. Pharmaceutical efficacy claims are less reliable because companies control the research, publication bias suppresses negative results, and financial incentives favor overstating benefits. Neither deserves blind trust or blanket dismissal; they deserve skepticism proportional to their historical reliability and structural incentives.

Calibration means updating your beliefs based on outcome tracking. When you believe something, make a note of your confidence level and what would cause you to change your mind, then check back later to see if you were right. This is uncomfortable because it forces confrontation with your own fallibility, but it's the only way to improve accuracy over time. Most people never do this; they remember their successful predictions and forget their failures, maintaining inflated confidence in their judgment. Deliberate tracking reveals how often you're wrong, which domains you're reliably right about versus consistently mistaken in, and whether your confidence matches your accuracy. If you're 90 percent confident in your predictions but only right 60 percent of the time, you're overconfident and need to dial back your certainty. If you're 60 percent confident but right 90 percent of the time, you're underconfident and can trust your judgment more. Neither feels natural. Overconfidence is comfortable; uncertainty is anxious. But calibration isn't about comfort, it's about aligning your internal sense of certainty with external reality, so you stop being so catastrophically wrong while feeling so completely right.

The practical application means developing different trust levels for other domains. I trust NASA's technical competence with spacecraft engineering at maybe 95 percent. They have excellent track records, strong feedback loops, and failures are highly visible and investigated. I trust nutrition science at maybe 40 percent; the field is plagued by weak methodology, contradictory findings, industry funding, and complexity that makes simple recommendations impossible. I trust the FDA's drug approval process at maybe 70 percent, better than nothing, sometimes captured by industry interests, but generally preventing the worst poisons from reaching the market. These numbers aren't precise; they're rough heuristics that help me weight evidence appropriately. When NASA says something about orbital mechanics, I accept it unless presented with very strong contradicting evidence. When a nutritionist makes claims about an optimal diet, I treat it as an interesting hypothesis requiring substantial verification. This doesn't mean nihilism; it means refusing to treat all knowledge claims as equally reliable and demanding that sources earn trust through demonstrated accuracy rather than receiving it automatically through credentials or institutional affiliation.

The Social Costs of Truth-Seeking

Nobody tells you that getting better at detecting BS makes you insufferable at parties. Your friend shares an inspiring story about someone who cured their cancer with positive thinking, and you're the asshole who brings up survivorship bias and spontaneous remission rates. Your uncle forwards an article about how the government is hiding free energy technology, and you're the one who has to explain why thermodynamics makes that impossible and ruins Thanksgiving. Your colleague repeats a viral claim about how a certain food causes autism, and you're the pedant who digs up the retracted study and the journalist who fabricated the data. Every conversation becomes an opportunity for correction, and correction makes people defensive. They didn't want accuracy; they wanted connection. The inspiring story wasn't about oncology; it was about hope. The conspiracy theory wasn't about energy policy; it was about feeling like you understand what the elites don't want you to know. The health claim wasn't about autism; it was about feeling like you're protecting your children through knowledge. By insisting on factual accuracy, you're missing the emotional function these narratives serve.

This creates a genuine dilemma. Do you let misinformation spread because correcting it damages relationships? Do you stay silent when someone shares claims that are demonstrably false but emotionally meaningful to them? The truth-seeker's instinct is to fix, but correction often fails while simultaneously alienating the person you're trying to help. Research on effective debiasing shows that direct contradiction tends to strengthen false beliefs through a phenomenon called the "backfire effect." People dig into their position harder when challenged. The alternative approach, asking questions rather than asserting corrections, expressing curiosity about their reasoning, and guiding them toward discovering contradictions themselves, works better but requires enormous patience and often still fails. Most people aren't looking for truth; they're looking for narrative coherence and tribal belonging. The truth-seeker ends up isolated, stuck between the community that believes comfortable fictions and the impossibility of pretending not to notice those fictions. You can't unsee BS once you've learned to recognize it but seeing it clearly doesn't give you the power to make others see it. You just end up alone in clarity, watching everyone else bond over shared delusions.

The honest calculus is that truth-seeking makes you socially awkward, professionally disadvantaged, and perpetually uncertain while surrounded by people who are confident, successful, and wrong. The Bester who confidently asserts falsehoods gets promoted while you're stuck explaining why the question is complicated. The influencer who sells snake oil gets rich while you're writing substacks nobody reads, explaining why their product doesn't work. The politician who promises simple solutions wins elections while you're pointing out that policy trade-offs don't have easy answers. There's no reward structure for truth-seeking except internal, the satisfaction of believing things for good reasons, the integrity of refusing to participate in collective delusion, and the possibility that accuracy matters more than comfort. That's not nothing, but it's also not enough to convince most people that the trade-off is worth it. Truth-seeking is a voluntary affliction you take on despite incentives, not because of them. The fog is thick, and most people would rather stay lost together than struggle toward clarity alone. The person who insists on seeking truth anyway isn't heroic; they're stubborn, cursed with the inability to accept easy answers, unable to enjoy the comfort of certainty that comes from just believing what everyone else thinks. But they're the only ones who might eventually find a way through the fog, even if they can't convince anyone else to follow them through it.

About The Author

Taylor Reed is a social commentator and cultural critic renowned for their incisive analysis of contemporary societal issues. With a background in sociology and philosophy, they have spent years examining the complexities of communication and truth in the modern world. Reed's previous works have delved into themes of authenticity, representation, and the intersection of media and personal identity. Their unique perspective stems from a commitment to uncovering the underlying structures that guide human behavior in a rapidly changing landscape. Drawing on historical examples and the latest cultural phenomena, Reed aims to spark important conversations about the truths we accept and the deceptions we perpetuate. When not writing, Taylor is often found engaging in public speaking and workshops aimed at promoting critical thinking and media literacy.

About The Publisher

Welcome to The Book On Publishing

At The Book On Publishing, we believe in rewriting the rules of learning. Whether you're chasing your next big idea, building a better life, or simply curious about what should have been taught in school, you've come to the right place.

We're a platform built for dreamers, doers, and lifelong learners, offering bold, practical books and tools that empower you to take charge of your journey. From real-world skills to mindset mastery, we publish the book on what matters.

No fluff. No lectures. Just what you need to know, delivered with clarity, purpose, and a spark of curiosity.

Start exploring. Start growing. Start writing your story.

Read more at https://thebookon.ca.

Acknowledgment of AI Assistance

Portions of this book were developed with the support of AI. While every word has been carefully reviewed and refined by the author, AI served as a valuable tool for brainstorming, editing, and structuring ideas. Its assistance helped accelerate the creative process and clarify complex topics.